Relief Carving
WORKSHOP

Techniques, Projects & Patterns for the Beginner

Lora S. Irish

FOX CHAPEL
PUBLISHING

© 2013 by Lora S. Irish and Fox Chapel Publishing Company, Inc., East Petersburg, PA.

Relief Carving Workshop is an original work, first published in 2013 by Fox Chapel Publishing Company, Inc. The patterns contained herein are copyrighted by the author. Readers may make copies of these patterns for personal use. The patterns themselves, however, are not to be duplicated for resale or distribution under any circumstances. Any such copying is a violation of copyright law.

ISBN 978-1-56523-736-0

Library of Congress Cataloging-in-Publication Data

Irish, Lora S.

  Relief carving workshop : techniques, projects, and patterns for the beginner / Lora S. Irish.

    pages cm

  Summary: "If you'd like to learn to carve in relief, this comprehensive guidebook will teach you everything you need to know. Relief Carving Workshop takes you through every element of the relief carving process from start to finish. With some sharp tools, a smooth piece of wood and this new book, you'll soon be confidently carving exquisite animals, landscapes, flowers, borders, Celtic knots and more. Acclaimed carver and instructor Lora S. Irish takes you step-by-step through simple carvings on a practice board to introduce all of the essential cuts, contouring and smoothing steps used in basic relief woodcarving. The author reveals how easy it is to make each individual stroke, and shows how all relief carving is simply using these cuts over and over again. You'll learn how to handle your tools, prepare a wood surface, follow a pattern, and apply a finish. 10 original new project patterns are accompanied by clear in-depth instructions and dozens of how-to photographs. Each design is presented both as an outline pattern for tracing directly onto wood, and as a detailed sketch to guide your work. A stunning photo gallery of finished projects is included to offer further inspiration. With Basic Relief Woodcarving by your side, you'll swiftly develop skills to create beautiful carvings that can stand alone or enhance a wide variety of functional and decorative crafts. Inside you'll find everything you need to get started: - 10 New Project Patterns - Original Designs for Landscapes, Animals, Wildlife, Flowers, Borders, Corner Designs, Celtic Knots and more - Skill-Building Exercises - Guide to Basic Carving Tools - Proper Tool Handling Techniques - Selecting and Preparing Wood - Finishing with Oil, Wax and Acrylics -   A Stunning Gallery of Completed Projects "-- Provided by publisher.

  Includes index.

  ISBN 978-1-56523-736-0 (pbk.)

  1. Wood-carving--Technique. 2. Relief (Decorative arts) I. Title.

  TT199.7.I754 2013

  736'.4--dc23

                           2012033928

To learn more about the other great books from Fox Chapel Publishing, or to find a retailer near you, call toll-free 800-457-9112 or visit us at *www.FoxChapelPublishing.com*.

Note to Authors: We are always looking for talented authors to write new books. Please send a brief letter describing your idea to Acquisition Editor, 1970 Broad Street, East Petersburg, PA 17520.

Printed in Singapore
Second printing

About the Author

Lora S. Irish is an internationally known artist and author, whose acclaimed books include:

- *101 Artistic Relief Patterns*
- *Classic Carving Patterns*
- *Easy & Elegant Beaded Copper Jewelry*
- *Great Book of Celtic Patterns*
- *Great Book of Dragon Patterns*
- *Great Book of Fairy Patterns*
- *Great Book of Floral Patterns*
- *Great Book of Tattoo Designs*
- *Great Book of Woodburning*

- *Landscapes in Relief*
- *Modern Tribal Tattoo Designs*
- *North American Wildlife Patterns for the Scroll Saw*
- *Relief Carving Wood Spirits*
- *The Official Vampire Artist's Handbook*
- *Wildlife Carving in Relief*
- *Wood Spirits and Green Men*
- *World Wildlife Patterns for the Scroll Saw*

Lora S. Irish

In addition to her work as an author, in 1997, working from her home studio, Lora and her husband, Michael, created *www.carvingpatterns.com*, an Internet-based studio focusing on online tutorials, projects, and patterns created exclusively by Lora for crafters and artisans. The website offers more than 2,100 patterns in various subject categories, including Americana, Animal and Wildlife, Celtic Knots, Dragons and Beasts, Nautical and Sea Life, Spirit People, and many more. Lora continues to provide new patterns—and inspiration to many artists—at the site.

Lora also contributes a regular relief carving pattern column to *Woodcarving Illustrated* magazine and is a frequent contributor to *Scroll Saw Woodworking and Crafts* magazine.

Contents

PROJECTS

Introduction
Styles of Relief Woodcarving

Relief carving is the process of cutting a design or pattern into a flat surface; relief carving media include wood, stone, linoleum, clay, and synthetic carving blanks.

To create a raised, dimensional look in a relief carving design, the background area of the carving blank is lowered using chisels and gouges. The lower the background is carved into the blank, the higher the design area appears to be.

The design is then worked in small, grouped element sections called levels or layers, which include the background or sky area of the pattern, the mid-ground area, the foreground area, and the highest, foremost element. Each layer of a design is carved to set it down into the wood at a predetermined depth according to where it lies within the design.

The simplest form of relief carving is called *sgraffito*, meaning to scratch into the surface. Using the most basic tools of relief carving—the bench knife and V-gouge—a design can be created with thin, shallow cuts made across a flat surface.

Low relief carvings, also called bas-relief, use shallow changes of depth between the layers of the pattern elements and simple, rounded-over edges. The sidewalls of the elements within the design have vertical, smooth walls.

One of our carving projects, *Mayan High Priest*, is a low relief carving. The original Mayan carving of this pattern was worked in stone with minimal changes in the depth of each element. Yet the completed work gives a strong feeling of dimension that is accented by fine, tightly packed detail work.

High relief carvings are not necessarily cut deeper into the wood or stone. Instead, a technique called undercutting places the joint lines between two elements underneath the higher element. The walls of an element can roll in convex or concave curves, adding to the realism of the finished carving.

Some areas of a high relief carving can be cut to become freestanding areas within the design. A blade of grass or tree branch can be undercut to completely separate a portion of the blade or branch from the elements below. Undercutting adds large, dark shadows to the piece.

As you work through the pages of this book, you will discover a simple set of carving tools, a few sharpening stones, and a stack of carving blanks is all you need to create stunning relief work. We will explore how to prepare your wood blank, how to work with relief carving patterns, and the general steps used in any relief work.

Ancient Influence

The Aztec, Inca, and Mayan cultures left few artifacts and almost no paper writing through which we can learn of their religious, social, and political structures. Yet the treasure of their lives and societies can be found relief-carved into the stone ruins of their cities.

Their written languages were a complex set of pictorial images—hieroglyphs that have survived up to 5,500 years—detailing everything from simple daily routines to the intricate hereditary lines of rulers.

Originally carved into the limestone walls of temples, palaces, and even sports arenas, these hieroglyphs included many favorite carving themes seen in woodcraft today—animals, birds, plants, and for this woodcarving project, the Mayan High Priest Lord Bird Jaguar I of Mexico (circa 600–900 A.D.).

Lord Bird Jaguar I—Mayan High Priest

CHAPTER 1

Woodcarving
TOOLS

Carving tools are available packaged in pre-selected kits or as individual tools. Woodcarving has such a large variety of possible carving styles, wood, and techniques—each with its own specialty tool requirements—that it is difficult for the beginner to know which tools he or she will be using. I strongly recommend a basic tool kit for the new carver. As you grow in the craft, you can add to your basic kit those tools that will be most useful to you.

ASSEMBLING A BASIC TOOL KIT

A basic carving tool kit includes a bench knife, a large and small round gouge, a straight chisel, a skew chisel, and a V-gouge. As your interest in woodcarving grows, you may wish to add to your basic tool kit detail knives, wide sweep gouges, and a bull-nose chisel.

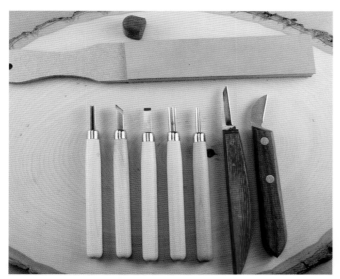

Basic beginner's carving kit from left: V-gouge, skew chisel, straight chisel, large round gouge, medium round gouge, bench knife, and a large chip carving knife. At top: leather strop and stropping compound.

Advanced beginner's carving kit. Interchangeable tool tip set: tight, medium, and large U-gouges; veining tool; V-gouge; straight chisel; wide, medium, and small sweep gouges; round gouge; chip carving knife; detail and bench knives; leather strop (not shown); and rouging compound (not shown).

Carving tool variables

Carving tools are available based on several factors—the shape of the handle, the size of the handle, the weight of the shaft and cutting edge, the cutting edge profile, the cutting edge angle or curve, and the profile of the metal shaft.

Handheld tools often have a short—less than 5" (127mm) long—handle, which can be ergonomic, palm-shaped, or thin and straight. The short handle allows for a firm grip within the palm of the hand and places the holding hand close to or directly onto the wood. All three styles of handle are available for interchangeable cutting blades.

Mallet tools have long, thick—5" (127mm) or greater—handles and are made to be used with a rubber, wood, or leather mallet. The metal shafts and cutting edges tend to be thicker than handheld tools to stand up to the force of the mallet blow. With this style of tool, the carving tool is held in one hand with the blade against the wood and the mallet held in the other as the mallet drives the tool's edge through the wood.

The cutting edge profile of woodcarving tools can be a straight-edged chisel, a rounded or curved-edge round gouge, or even a 90°-angled V-gouge. The profile of the cutting edge determines the shape of the cut in the wood. A wide-sweep gouge makes wide, shallow cuts in the wood, while tight round gouges make deep half-circle cuts.

The angle of the metal shaft of carving tools also varies. Most commonly, the shaft of a carving tool is straight, but tools can also have bent shafts that angle the cutting edge up or down from the centerline of the tool handle. Back-bent shafts drop the cutting profile so that the tool's edge can be used in tight areas. Angled bent shafts are called doglegs and drop the cutting edge flat against the surface of the wood.

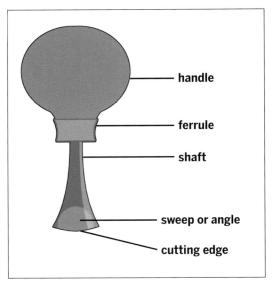

handle

ferrule

shaft

sweep or angle

cutting edge

Carving tools come in many different shapes and sizes. Any one of the labeled elements can vary from tool to tool.

Differences. Carving tools come in a variety of tool handle shapes and lengths. Palm handle tools are excellent for close detail work that needs total cutting control. Try a long-handled tool for rough out and shaping work. Long palm tool handles give both the control needed for fine line carving and the leverage for rough out work.

Wide-sweep, round, and U-gouges

Round gouges are sorted by the open or tight curve of the cutting profile. Wide, flat curves are called sweeps, medium-curved profiles are rounds, and tools with tight curves are called U-gouges.

Sweep gouges are often used to shape concave forms such as spoons or bowls. In relief carving, the wide-sweep gouge can also be used to clean ridges left by the roughing out steps.

For very tight areas within a carving, use a U-gouge. Its long, narrow shaft and the rounded bottom area of the profile are perfect for teasing out deep, tight areas.

A medium-round gouge can be up-ended—set onto the wood in an upright position so that just the cutting edge touches the wood. By applying light pressure to the tool, you can roll the cutting edge into an arc or circle to create rounded shapes like grapes, berries, and beads.

V-gouges and parting tools

The V-gouge, also called a parting tool, has a crisply angled cutting edge with two straight sides that create a V-shaped cut. The angle of the cutting profile ranges from very tight, narrow angles for fine detailing to wide, open angles for separating one area of a carving from another. The size of the cutting edge also varies from micro-V-gouges that have ⅛" (3mm)-high cutting sides to ½" (13mm)-high sides for mallet work. Most V-gouges found in beginner's tool kits have 90° angles.

Chisels: straight, skew, bull-nose, and bent-shaft

Straight chisels have straight, flat cutting edges used to round over and smooth curved edges in carvings. The straight cutting edges remove thin, long slivers of wood. The front or top side of the chisel is beveled toward the cutting edge with the back side flat to the shaft.

Skew chisels have the cutting edge slanted either to the left or right side of the chisel, allowing you to cut into tight corners. Bull-nose chisels are not true, straight-edged tools—instead their profile uses a gentle, rounded curve with no sharp points at the end of the cutting edge.

Most gouges, V-gouges, and chisels are available as bent-shaft tools. The arc or bend can vary from

Gouges. Top to bottom: flat wide-sweep gouge, medium wide-sweep gouge, small wide-sweep gouge, large U-gouge, medium U-gouge, and small U-gouge (also called a veining tool).

The V-gouge creates a crisp, sharp, angled trough in the wood.

Chisels. Left to right: palm handle interchangeable straight chisel, Japanese skew and straight chisel, rosewood long handle skew and bull-nose chisel, and bent-shaft bull-nose chisel.

a shallow curve to a deep turn in the shaft that allows you to drop the tool into low areas within your design.

Straight-blade knives: bench, chip carving, whittling, and detail

Straight-blade knives come under several different names determined by the length of the blade, the angle of the blade, and the use of the knife.

Bench knives have long, straight blades from 1¼"–1¾" (32–44mm) in length or longer. They are used for making stop cuts, shaping elements, and for general whittling steps in your work.

The short, angled blade of a chip carving knife places your cutting hand close to the wood. Chip carvings are made using small triangular cuts to create a larger geometric pattern. The short distance between the handgrip and the blade point make them excellent relief carving knives.

Whittling knives come in a variety of lengths, blade widths, and cutting edge profiles. The example shown has a short, 1¼" (32mm)-long, straight blade with a detail style point at the tip with a hand-formed grip that makes it very comfortable for long periods of work.

Small straight knives with fine, thin points are called detail knives. The three shown all have short blades, each less than ¾" (19mm) long. The inside profile of the cutting edge can be horizontal to the knife's grip, angled, or curved.

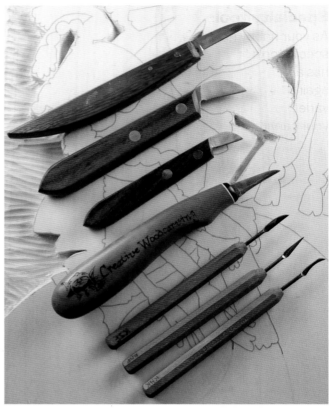

Knives. Top to bottom: bench knife, large chip carving knife, small chip carving knife, whittling knife, straight detail knife, fine point detail knife, and concave detail knife.

Using Straight-blade Knives

Straight-blade knives are made for cutting, not for prying or digging into the wood. No matter how tempting, do not use the point of a straight knife to pop out a small corner chip—doing so will break the fine, thin point. Instead use a small U-gouge to remove those tightly enclosed bits of wood.

If you do snap the point of any tool, you will need to re-grind the cutting profile on a coarse sharpening stone.

Specialty tools

As your hobby grows, you may want to add a few special tools to your basic set. The dogleg chisel has a bent shaft that allows you to lay the chisel flat against the wood surface. Detail knives come in a variety of curved profiles made to fit the curve of your carving.

Other tool kit supplies

A few common household items will complete your carving kit. Scissors, tape, pens and pencils, rulers, and dusting brushes are just a few of the supplies that are needed during any carving session.

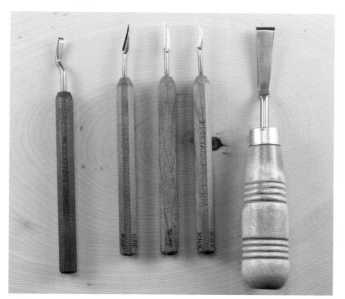

Tool kit expansion. Left to right: dogleg chisel, skew detail knife, straight detail knife, curved detail knife, and large dogleg chisel.

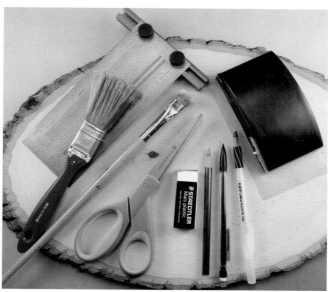

Miscellaneous supplies. General items for your carving kit include a soft #2 pencil for pattern changes, ink pens for pattern tracing, scissors, dusting brushes or a toothbrush, sandpaper and sanding pads, a T-square and rulers, and a white artist eraser.

TOOL STORAGE

By separating each knife in your kit you protect the cutting edge of the tool. Tools thrown loosely in an open box can have their cutting edges dented by rolling or hitting another tool. Cloth and leather wraps are available that have sewn pockets for each tool in your kit. Avoid, if possible, storing your tools in closed plastic sleeves or plastic bags, as this can trap moisture that will cause rust.

Storage. This simple knife storage box is made from a wooden craft box. The bottom of the box has been lined with tag board that has been folded to create individual storage spaces.

WORKING SURFACES

You do not need a dedicated workshop or even a worktable to enjoy relief woodcarving. One of my favorite places to carve is in the living room as I enjoy an evening with my family.

Any secure, non-moveable surface can be used as a carving table. For evening carving sessions, I use a strong kitchen chair, anchored by non-skid mats under each leg. The chair's seat creates a worktable with the chair back as a stop.

Using a bench hook

Another way to secure a carving as you work is with a bench hook. The bench hook is a simple and easy carving jig that will become an indispensable asset to your relief carving, allowing you to anchor or brace your projects while using a gouge or skew.

To use a bench hook, drop the front edge over the edge of your worktable and slip the carving project into the corner brace. As you push each carving stroke, the front edge of the bench hook grabs against the table edge and keeps your carving project from sliding away from the stroke. You can quickly flip and turn your carving project to be braced in the corner of the jig for each cut you make.

I place a terrycloth towel under the bench hook. I often carve in the rec room or living room, and the towel protects whatever table I am using and collects the wood chips for easy cleanup later.

The simple bench hook pictured was made using scraps of ½" (13mm)-thick plywood and ¾" (19mm)-thick pine. An 8" x 16" (203 x 406mm) piece of plywood makes up the base. Two 3" x 7" (76 x 178mm) boards were added along the back edge and side of the base to create a corner brace. An 8" x 2" (203 x 51mm) scrap was secured to the front of the base, creating the front edge to grip the edge of your work surface and keep the bench hook from moving.

Note: As a left-handed carver, I placed my corner brace in the upper right-hand side of my bench hook. As I cut—moving my tool from left to right—I push into that corner. If you are a right-handed carver, place your corner brace on the left side of your bench hook. See the instructions on the next page to create your own bench hook.

Keeping wood in place. Non-skid mats, heavy terrycloth towels, and even corkboard squares hold the carving wood to the work surface.

Making a bench hook

Use the supplies and instructions below to create your own bench hook to use for your relief carving projects.

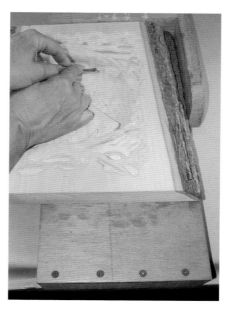

Bench hook. This simple plywood bench hook secures the corner of your carving blank, allowing you to safely make your cuts without the blank moving on the table.

1 Use four wood screws to attach the front brace board to the bottom front edge of your base. Make sure you place the screws perpendicular to the base floor so that you will be pushing against the screws while carving, not with the screws. This will prevent them from "walking out" of the wood over time and use.

2 Attach one of the corner brace boards along the back top edge of the base, again making sure you place the screws perpendicular to the base floor. With the two boards attached, your bench hook should have a "Z" shape.

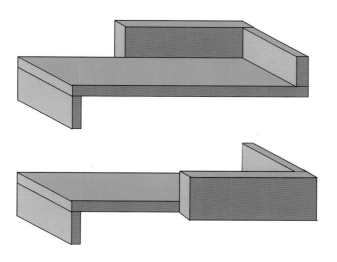

3 If you are right handed, attach the second corner brace board along the left side of the top of the base. If you are left handed, attach the board along the right side of the top corner.

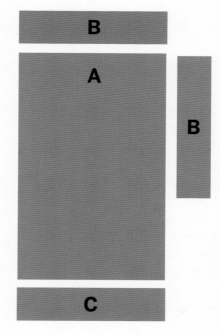

Supplies

- **Base (A):** One ½" (13mm)-thick plywood board, 8" x 16" (203 x 406mm)
- **Corner brace (B):** Two ¾" (19mm)-thick pine boards, 3" x 7" (76 x 178mm)
- **Front brace (C):** One ¾" (19mm)-thick pine board, 8" x 2" (203 x 52mm)
- **Assembly pieces:** Sixteen 1¼" (32mm)-long wood screws

CHAPTER 2

Sharpening CARVING TOOLS

Sharpening tools are as important to a carving kit as cutting tools. The cutting edge of any tool needs to be kept as sharp as possible to create clean, even strokes. A dull tool will leave fine scratch lines, giving the finished stroke a dull, coarse texture. Dull tools are also much more dangerous than sharpened ones. An unsharpened tool requires you to use more force to create the desired cut, making it easy for you to lose control and let the tool slip.

Keep carving tools sharp. A sharpening kit includes stones of various grits, emery cloth, leather or synthetic strops, and honing/roughing compounds.

TYPES OF SHARPENING TOOLS

There are many tools and supplies you can use to sharpen your carving tools. Sharpening stones, including natural stones like the Arkansas stone, clay-based stones like the Japanese water stone, and man-made stones like the white and brown ceramic stones, are commonly used among carvers.

Because of their large working surfaces, I like to use my Japanese water stones on my large tools—1" (25mm) or wider. In my tool kit, though, I always carry a set of ceramic stones. Ceramic stones can be used dry or with water, and they retain their flat, even surfaces even after many years of use. They are small, palmed-sized stones, making them very easy to use.

A few assorted sharpening tools.

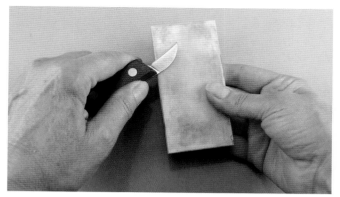

Sharpening stones are available in 800 to 1000 grits, used for beveling the blade, and fine grits—up to 8000—used for sharpening.

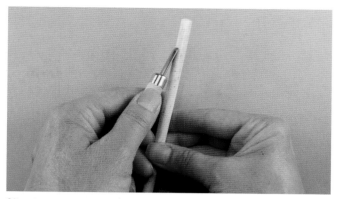

Slip stones come in a variety of profiles to fit V-gouges and round gouges.

You should clean your sharpening stones using dishwashing soap and water when they begin to take on a blackish hue from the metal grindings.

Emery cloth (silicon oxide sanding paper) is also useful for keeping tools sharp. It comes in extremely fine grits—from 1200 down—and is made for metal working and polishing. This sanding cloth is readily available at your local hardware store.

When using emery cloth, secure it to a strong, flat surface to keep the cloth from moving as you sharpen your blades.

The honing strop is probably the most important sharpening tool at your disposal. Made of leather or synthetic material and used with a honing/roughing compound, a strop removes the waste steel that can be left on a blade after sharpening with a coarse and fine stone, giving a fine, smooth polish to your tool's edge.

Rouging compounds are available as a yellow compound, a green compound, a red oxide, and an aluminum oxide powder.

Clean the rawhide side of your leather strop when it becomes black and encrusted by scraping the surface with a dull-edged table knife. Saddle soap can be used for the tanned leather side of the strop.

Emery cloth is an extremely fine-grit sandpaper available at your local hardware store.

The leather strop and a roughing compound, staples in a carving kit, are used to hone the edges of any tool.

Slip strops have contoured areas made for easy sharpening of V-gouges and round gouges.

BASIC SHARPENING TECHNIQUES

There are as many techniques for sharpening your tools as there are styles of tool sharpening systems. Each carver seems to have a system by which he or she can create a fine edge on all his or her tools. The system you use will be determined by its ability to allow you to repeatedly create the sharp cutting edges on your tools needed for relief carving.

There are a few guidelines you should follow, no matter what sharpening tool or system you plan to use:

1. Use a coarse sharpening stone when your tool has severe dents or dings, including small areas of damage to the cutting edge that often appear as bright spots along the blade. Only use a coarse stone when necessary, as it will destroy the working edge your tool currently has.

2. If you tool is not severely damaged and only needs to have the cutting edge refreshed, use a fine stone.

3. Complete any sharpening session using a honing strop covered with honing/roughing compound. Work both sides of your tool's edge on the strop. During a carving session, hone often, about every half hour; just a few pulls across the strop will retain your tool's sharp cutting edge as you work.

4. When using a honing strop, pull your tool across the strop in a backward motion, away from the cutting edge. Lift the tool, turn it over to the back, place the back against the honing strop, and pull.

5. When sharpening, do not flip or roll your tool. Instead, use a pull-lift-reposition-pull action. Flipping or rolling the tool over will round the cutting edge.

SIMPLE STEPS TO SHARPENING

Here are the basic steps to creating tools that are razor sharp.

1 **Start with a coarse stone.** Begin your sharpening session by working the tool's edge on a coarse stone, like the 800-grit Japanese water stone shown here. Water or fine-grade oil can be used as a lubricant depending on the style of stone you are using—be sure to refer to the manufacturer's suggestions. Ceramic stone can be used dry. Place the edge of the tool on the stone, and then pull the tool across the stone's surface, away from the cutting edge. Work both the front and back of the tool. You can also use a circular motion to shape the edge. Coarse stones create the general bevel or shape of the tool. Continue to work with the coarse stone until any dents or rough areas along the cutting edge of the tool have been removed (about five minutes).

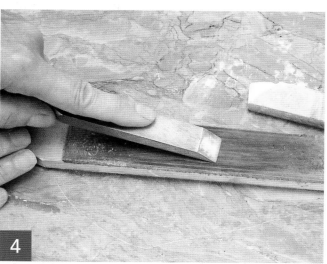

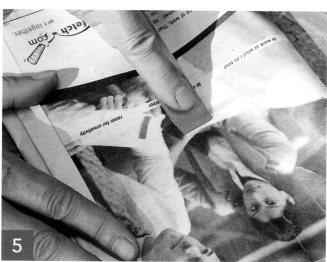

2 **Move to a fine stone.** Move your tool to a fine sharpening stone, like the 6000-grit Japanese water stone pictured. A fine stone removes any ridges left after working with the coarse stone and smooths the tool's cutting profile. Work on the fine stone for about five minutes.

3 **Check the tool's edge.** The pulling motion used when working on the coarse and fine stones works a very thin layer of steel from the cutting edge of the tool. This layer, called a tin edge, can be seen in this photo as a fine white line on the cutting edge.

4 **Hone the edge.** If you run your finger from the back of the blade toward the front, you will feel the tin edge. This edge is removed using a leather or synthetic strop and a honing/roughing compound. Rub a layer of roughing compound over the rawhide side of a leather strop. Place the tool's edge against the rawhide and pull away from the cutting edge. Hone your tool until the tin edge has been released from the edge of the blade. Turn the leather honing strop over to the tanned hide side and, without applying roughing compound to the strop, continue to dress the edge of the blade.

5 **Give a final polish.** Polish the full surface of your tool by pulling it across a folded, heavily printed sheet of newspaper.

CHAPTER 3

Selecting
CARVING WOOD

Basswood is the perfect beginner's carving wood. It is available through mail order in board form and as pre-routed shaped blanks in many craft stores. Basswood, although classified as a hardwood, has a soft carving surface. Because each wood has its own carving properties, the projects throughout this book are worked exclusively on basswood to allow you, the new carver, to learn how to use your tools and control your cuts before you begin carving with other wood species.

As your skills grow you may also use black walnut, butternut, mahogany, soft maple, or sugar pine.

COMMON CARVING WOODS

Basswood (*Tilia americana*), also called American Lime. Basswood is a soft, creamy white wood that is easy to work and glues into large blocks very well. It has no figuring, with a fine, straight, even grain, and the sapwood is almost white. Basswood carves well and is excellent for detail work. Very lightweight, basswood is used in carving, turning, and toy making.

Basswood

Butternut (*Juglans cinerea*), also called White Walnut. Much lighter in weight than black walnut, this wood has a medium, fine, straight grain with a golden brown tone that becomes reddish brown at the sapwood. If you use an oil finish on a butternut carving, the surface takes on a light oak tone. Butternut is excellent for high relief with some fine detailing, and is used in furniture carving and veneering.

Butternut

Red Cedar

Cypress

Red Cedar (*Juniperus virginiana*) also called Eastern Red Cedar, Red Juniper, or Pencil Cedar. Native to Canada and the Gulf of Mexico, red cedar has a mahogany to maroon-purple heartwood color with paler growth rings. It has distinguished grain lines and is a soft carving wood, although it can be brittle.

Yellow Cedar (*Thuja occidentalis*), also called American Arborvitae, Atlantic White Cedar, and False Cedar. Although referred to as a cedar, this wood is from the cypress family (cypress wood shown in photograph) and has the same carving qualities as red cedar.

Cherry

Cherry (*Prunus* and *Prunus avium*), also called Wild Cherry. A species commonly found throughout North America, Europe, and Asia, this hardwood has a wonderful, deep red heartwood surrounded by golden red growth rings.

Jelutong

Jelutong (*Dyera costulata*). A soft wood much like butternut, jelutong has a silvery gray sheen when finished. It is fine-textured and straight-grained. Jelutong often contains sap channels throughout the wood, but these can add to the mystique of a carving created from it. It is used in carving and pattern making.

Mahogany

Mahogany (*Swietenia macrophylla*). Mahogany has a reddish tone that deepens beautifully over time. It is a strong yet lightweight wood with a straight and even grain. Mahogany shaves well and takes extremely fine detail. It is used in furniture making, veneers, carving, and turn work.

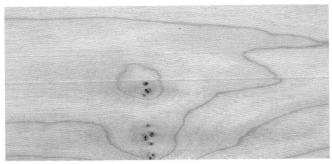
Soft Maple

Obeche

Soft Maple (*Acer saccharinum*), also called Water Maple or White Maple. A fast-growing maple commonly found in eastern North America, this hardwood cuts cleanly and has a pure white coloring to the wood.

Obeche (*Triplochiton scleroxylon*), also called Wawa. Extremely soft with a featureless grain, obeche is easily indented with any pressure and requires careful treatment in pattern tracing and handling. Carving knives need to be finely honed for the best cutting strokes in this wood. Obeche is exceptionally lightweight and used in model making and three-dimensional carving.

Sassafras

Sassafras (*Sassafras albidum*). A hardwood similar to walnut in its ability to be carved, sassafras has a very interesting, distinct grain pattern that is straight. The wood has a medium to heavy weight and is creamy tan with darker brown grain lines. It is used in furniture making, furniture carving, and carving.

Walnut

Walnut (*Juglans nigra*), also called Black Walnut and American Walnut. Walnut is an extremely durable wood that works well for relief carving. Most walnut carving work is done with a chisel and mallet. The grain is medium-coarse, yet straight. Walnut burls can have very interesting figuring within them. The color of walnut can change quickly from deep reddish brown to creamy white. It is used in furniture making, furniture carving, turning, and carving.

Toxic Woods

Most common carving woods are safe, but some woods are toxic, while others can cause skin irritation and respiratory problems. Before carving any variety of wood, research its safety, potential toxicity, and handling instructions to ensure your project is a healthy one.

Use a dust mask when sanding any wood to avoid breathing in the fine wood particles. Wash your hands often to remove any residue sap or dust from your wood. If you believe you are having a health-related issue during any carving session, seek medical assistance immediately.

EVALUATING WOOD GRAIN

The grain of your carving wood can affect your ability to create even, smooth cuts. It also directly determines the direction of your cuts.

Each year of new growth a tree experiences creates a new layer of grain. Tightly grained woods like basswood and butternut are excellent carving media.

Most woodcarving blanks are cut along the length or height of the tree, creating long grain lines. You can also obtain end grain cuts that are made by cutting the blank across the width of the tree.

Heartwood is found in the center of the tree and often has wider grain lines and a darker coloring than the outer growth rings.

Straight grain wood

End grain wood

Heartwood

SELECTING WOOD BLANKS

Quality wood creates quality carvings. When selecting carving blanks, look for clean, blemish-free wood with no signs of cupping or warping. The photo to the right shows an end grain round basswood blank and a straight grain basswood blank. You can find basswood carving blanks at most large craft stores or order your wood online through a mail-order wood supplier.

Wood blanks are available in varying widths from ¾"–4" (19–102mm) thick. The depth of the wood determines the depth of your carving. Most one-piece blanks range from 4"–12" (102–305mm) wide. Larger blanks are created by gluing several boards together to create the final width.

Basswood blanks. Basswood is an excellent wood for relief carving. Although it is classified as a hardwood, its even, fine grain is easy to cut. The clean white coloring of basswood takes any media of paint well.

BASIC GUIDE TO MAIL-ORDER WOOD

Not every carver is lucky enough to have a source of excellent carving woods close at hand. Although it is ideal to be able to browse the local lumber or carving supply store and handpick the next blank for a project, most carvers need to obtain their wood from a lumber supplier that will ship it to their homes. Such businesses are also an option if there is a special type of wood you wish to use that just is not available to you at local stores. Through mail-order lumber suppliers, you can find domestic and imported woods, softwoods and hardwoods, and even exotic woods that can be delivered right to your door.

In my experience, these wood suppliers are extremely helpful in guiding new carvers in selecting wood and will answer any questions you may have about what to order and how to determine how much wood you will need. Continue reading for a list of common terms you will need to know for the mail-order process.

Common mail-order terms

Board foot: This is the standard unit of measurement for wood, the unit being one foot long, one foot wide, and one inch thick. To determine the board foot measurement of your wood order, multiply the length of the board by the width of the board. Then, multiply your answer by the thickness of the board. Divide this answer by 144 (the number of square inches in a square foot). See the example below for a sample calculation.

S2S (surfaced two sides): This means both faces of a board have been milled, but the edges are not finished and will have a rough-sawn surface.

S4S (surfaced four sides): An S4S board has been milled on both faces as well as on both edges.

4/4, 5/4, 6/4, and 8/4: These numbers represent the thickness of a board as measured in quarter inches. A 4/4 board (or 4 quarter inches) is 1" thick, a 5/4 board (or 5 quarter inches) is 1¼" thick, a 6/4 board is 1½" thick, and an 8/4 board is 2" thick.

Short packs: Most mail-order wood suppliers will provide you with short packs. These are usually sold in predetermined amounts of board feet, such as a 20-board foot short pack or a 50-board foot short pack. These packs contain a variety of widths, lengths, and thicknesses of the same species of wood. Short packs are an excellent way to purchase wood if you are a beginner who does not have a specific project in mind but wishes to have carving wood on hand.

Selected sizes: This is wood that is ordered in a specific length, width, and thickness. If you are working on a particular project that requires wood of specific dimensions, you will order your wood supplies in selected sizes. This wood will cost a bit more than the wood available in short packs, but it will also be milled and cut exactly as you need it.

AD (air-dried) wood: This is stock that has been stacked and allowed to dry naturally over a long period of time.

KD (kiln-dried) wood: Kiln-dried stock is heat-treated in either a gas-fired kiln or solar kiln to speed the drying process. Kiln-dried wood has less moisture content than air-dried wood—usually about 6–12 percent moisture content as compared to the 12–18 percent moisture content common in air-dried wood.

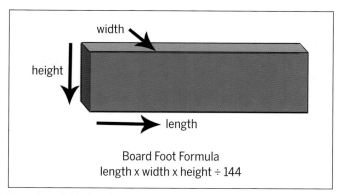

Board Foot Formula
length x width x height ÷ 144

Board foot. Mail-order wood is calculated by the board foot with 1 board foot being equal to 144 square inches.

Example

To calculate the board foot measurement of a board that is two feet long, three inches wide, and one inch thick:

Multiply the length by the width	24" x 3" = 72"
Then, multiply this answer by the thickness	72" x 1" = 72"
Divide this answer by 144	72"/144 = 0.5 board feet

CHAPTER 4

Working with
PATTERNS

Relief carving patterns not only carry the general outline of each area you will carve, but also all the necessary detailing and accent lines. If you trace the entire pattern onto your wood blank, most of your tracing lines will be cut away during the early carving steps. To prevent this, let's look at a few simple steps you can use to reduce your patterns to their simplest form, with the most basic information that you will need to trace onto your board. You will note that all the patterns in this book have been color coded to make tracing easy. Use this chapter to simplify patterns for any additional relief carvings you wish to do.

SIMPLIFYING A PATTERN

Follow these steps to reduce your pattern to the simplest element outlines.

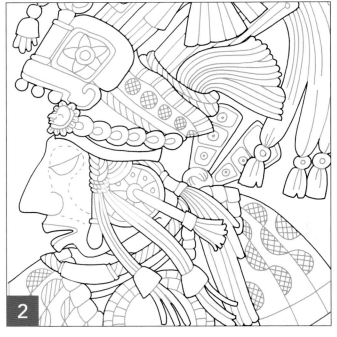

1 **Assess your pattern.** It is important to recognize that relief patterns not only include the general outline of your design, but also the fine finishing details.

2 **Outline the pattern elements.** To reduce a relief pattern to the basic lines needed for the very first carving steps, draw an outline along the outer edge of each element in the pattern. In this example, the front parts of the headdress have been grouped so they are defined as one element.

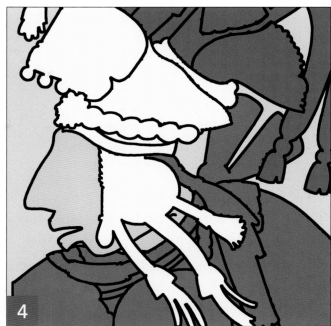

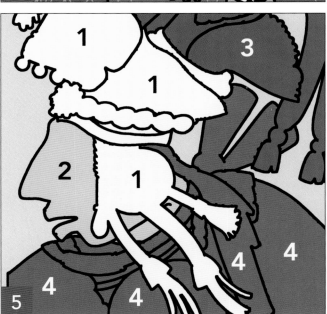

3 **Color each element.** In this example, I colored each element grouping, creating a pattern made up of individual elements instead of fine line details.

4 **Group and recolor the elements as desired.** To further simplify the design you can group the elements according to where they lie in the pattern, or group related elements together. For example, here the hair and hair ornament, shown in dark brown, are grouped into one larger element.

5 **Number the pattern based on depth.** Number each group of elements on your pattern according to their depth within the final design. For this pattern, I marked the highest area of the design as one, the high mid-ground as two, the low mid-ground as three, and the background elements as four.

6 **Trace the pattern.** When you have simplified the pattern and grouped the elements into their specific levels, you are ready to trace the outline of each grouping onto your carving blank. During the rough out steps, each grouping can be carved to its depth and then shaped.

TRACING A PATTERN

There are several ways to transfer a pattern to a carving blank. The instructions on page 27 use carbon paper, but graphite paper and pencil rubbing are also ways to easily transfer a pattern to wood.

Graphite paper. This paper is lightweight with a waxed graphite coating on one side. When tracing a pattern, the graphite side is placed against the wood, resulting in a tracing with medium-gray colored lines. Graphite paper is available in sheets as small 8½" x 11" (216 x 279mm) and as large as 48" x 96" (1219 x 2438mm), and also comes in rolls several yards long. Graphite paper can be used several times, so keep previously used pieces for later tracings.

Carbon paper. Originally used to make multiple copies of a typed or written document, carbon paper comes in black or dark blue. Tracings made using this product have heavy, dark, bold lines. Carbon paper is perfect for transferring patterns for long-term projects, as the traced lines will not fade or rub off, even after many hours of carving work.

Pencil rubbing. To use the pencil rubbing method for transferring a pattern, rub a soft #2 to #6 pencil over the back of your pattern paper. The higher the number of your pencil, the darker or blacker the rubbing will be. Then, place the pattern face up on your carving blank and begin tracing it. As you trace along the pattern lines, a thin, light gray coating of pencil will be left on the wood blank. Pencil rubbing lines can be erased using a white artist's eraser, making this an excellent method for transferring patterns for carvings that will include some pyrography work.

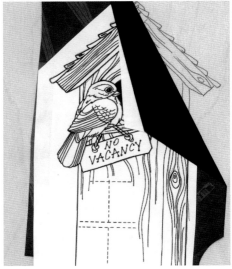

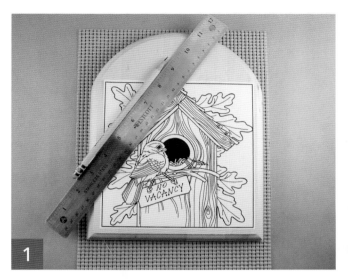

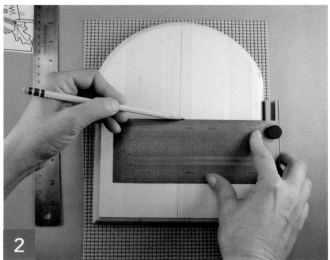

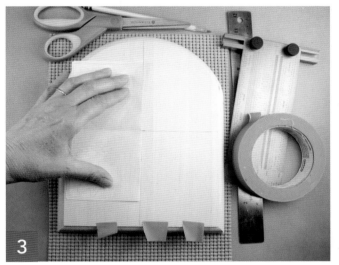

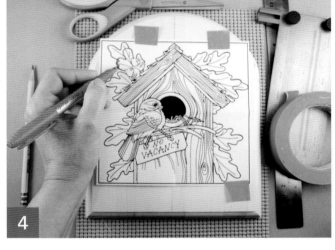

Simple steps for tracing a pattern

Tracing a pattern onto your carving blank is an important step; you want to make sure you center the pattern on the wood. Follow these steps to trace a pattern using carbon paper.

1 **Gather your supplies.** To transfer a pattern to your wood blank, you will need a copy of the pattern, carbon paper, an ink pen, a ruler, a T-square, a pencil, and tape.

2 **Mark the center of the blank.** Using your ruler and T-square, mark the center of the carving blank using a horizontal centerline and a vertical centerline.

3 **Align the pattern with the centerlines.** Fold the copy of the pattern into quarters. Place the pattern on the blank, aligning the fold lines in the paper with the centerlines drawn on the blank. Tape the pattern into place.

4 **Place the carbon paper, and trace.** Mark any adjustments necessary on your pattern. Slide the carbon paper in place under the pattern paper, and trace along the outside lines of your grouped elements.

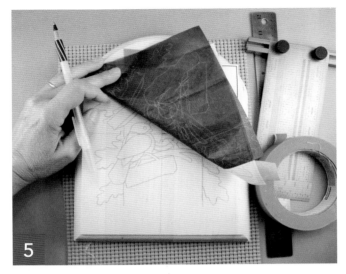

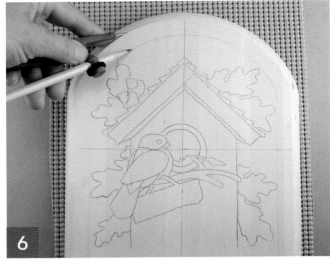

5 **Check your progress.** Check your tracing before you remove the pattern and carbon paper to ensure you have transferred all the necessary pattern lines.

6 **Create a border if desired.** If you like, you can use a compass to create an outside border or margin line around the pattern.

7 **Add in the details as you carve.** As you progress through the carving stages, cut small pieces of your original pattern paper, secure them to your wood blank, and trace the fine line details into those roughly cut areas.

PREPARING TO CARVE

Before you begin any relief carving project, make sure you do the following:

Remove jewelry. Remove all rings, bracelets, and long, hanging necklaces that could become caught on a tool tip before you begin carving.

Tie back long hair. If you have long hair, use a hairband to secure it. Long hair can easily block your view of the tool tip and cut.

Wear shoes. Dropped carving tools fall point down, and the top of your foot is the most likely object to be hit.

Check your workspace. If you sit while carving, check the seat of your chair for tools or interchangeable tool tips before you sit down again. Make it a habit to keep your tools on a nearby table or neatly laid beside your wood blank where they are always in view.

Secure the blank. Secure your carving blank using a terrycloth towel, nonslip mat, bench hook, or clamps. Well-secured blanks require less hand pressure to make cuts.

Lay out a towel. A terrycloth towel on your lap or on the floor will catch your waste chips. Check the towel for dropped tools before you dispose of the chips.

Take tool inventory. Count your tools during any cleanup sessions to ensure that you do not accidentally lose one.

Make a kit. Create a carving kit with all of the common tools and supplies you will use for any type of carving—carving tools, tracing paper, scissors, ruler, masking tape, pencil, sharpening tools, and any other tools or supplies you feel you might need. Creating a kit means you will have everything you need on hand so you can spend your time carving instead of searching for a tool that may or may not have been misplaced.

Cover your nails. Long fingernails can leave small dents in softer woods like basswood and butternut. A quilter's plastic thimble can be used to protect both your nails and your project without interfering with your hand movements.

Carving extras: gloves, thumb guards, and carving mats

Several styles of carving gloves, made of both leather and Kevlar, are available. You can also purchase a thumb guard made to cover the tip to the first joint of your thumb or finger during a carving session. These are especially designed for three-dimensional carving where you are holding the wood in one hand while using a carving tool in the other.

Most relief carvings are done on large wood blanks that are supported either on a carving table, worktable, or in your lap, and most relief carving strokes are made with a tool held in both hands. Seldom will you find yourself holding the carving blank in your hand, creating the potential for cuts. Because of this, carving gloves and thumb guards are not necessary for relief carving.

To protect yourself during a lap-carving session, place a heavy terrycloth towel, folded into quarters, over your legs.

The inevitable cut finger

Small cuts and slices are inevitable during woodcarving. It takes only one slip to land the cutting edge of a tool in a fingertip or the palm of your hand. Because of this, I do keep several absorbent gauze pads and butterfly bandages in my carving kit, just in case.

If you do cut your hand, use a sterile absorbent gauze pad to apply pressure to the cut area until the bleeding stops. Clean the cut with water and use an antibiotic cream on the cut before applying a bandage. If the cut is large or deep, please visit your doctor or the emergency room to have the cut stitched.

During twenty years of relief woodcarving, I have only once needed stitches, and that was for a small ¾" slice across the top of my finger. My cut came not from a carving stroke, but from reaching for a tool on my table. I had allowed my tools to pile up on my terrycloth towel and only glanced to see where the tool I wanted lay, so I cut my finger on the tip of the tool next to the one I wanted to grab. Today, I am careful to look before I reach.

Where to carve

As mentioned previously, some woodcarvers have an area in their workshop or basement set aside for carving, but many do not have an area that can be dedicated solely to carving. I personally prefer to do my relief carving in my home's rec room.

For small carvings, I work the project in my lap with a heavy terrycloth towel over my legs to protect myself from possible cuts, catch the waste chips, and make cleanup after a carving session easy. I keep the tools I am using during any session on a nearby end table.

When working on large projects, I spread an extra-large, heavy terrycloth towel on the floor in front of my workspace. Next, I set a sturdy wooden chair or small end table so it is facing my work seat. My rec room is carpeted, which keeps the towel/chair combination secure—if you have wooden or linoleum flooring you may need to place non-slip mats on the floor first.

I place a nonslip pad on the seat of the chair or top of the end table to secure my wood blank during carving. The chair seat is just the right height for me to easily and comfortably carve, while the back of the chair acts as a stop against the back edge of the wood blank.

Tool protection

Sharp tool tips create clean cuts, so you will want to protect those tips and keep them sharp as long as possible. Do not throw tools into a box where they can become dented or dull.

Because carving tools are created from steel, they can rust. Tools should be stored in a location that keeps moisture away from their tips. Tightly sealed tool wraps, especially plastic ones, trap moisture that can destroy the metal shafts and tips of your tools, so avoid tightly sealed or tight, form-fitting tool covers. Any natural product such as leather, cardboard, or paper absorbs moisture from the air that can condense on your tools, so avoid tightly sealed or tight, form fitting tool covers. Check that your tool covers have room for the tool to move and breathe.

Any tool storage system you utilize should keep each tool separate from the other tools in your kit, yet also provide air space and air movement around the tool tips. For long-term storage, you can apply a light coat of petroleum oil over any metal areas of your tools—ferrule, shaft, and tip. The oil can be removed by wiping the tool with a clean, lint-free cloth when you are ready to use it again.

Working with the wood grain

Before you begin carving, it is important to recognize that, whether you are using a chisel, bench knife, or chip carving knife to create your rounded-over edge, you need to work your tools with the direction of the wood's grain.

Working with the grain lines allows your tool to cut the wood, while working against the grain causes your tool's edge to catch between grain lines, causing the edge to dig deeply into the wood at that point.

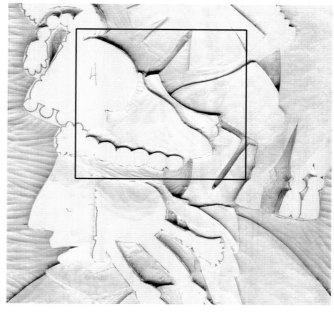

This photo of the Mayan High Priest project (page 70) was taken during the early stage of work where I rough out the levels. The section marked with the square is the area used for the close-up photos that follow.

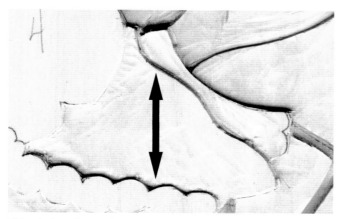

This photo is focused on the center point of the hat area of the carving. The grain for the carving blank runs vertically through the wood.

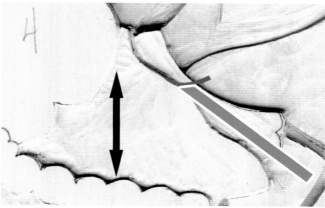

Carving with the grain means running your blade uphill along the grain edge. This removes a fine sliver of wood from the top of the wood grain.

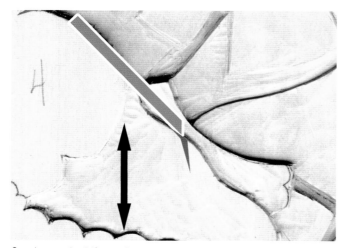

Carving against the grain means running your blade downhill into the fine separations between each grain line. This splits the wood along the grain lines, causing the blade to dig into the wood.

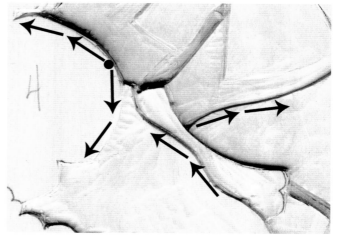

To cut many of the curves found in a relief carving, you will need to change the direction of your cutting blade several times to ensure you remain working with the grain of the wood.

CHAPTER 5

Creating a
PRACTICE BOARD

An easy way to learn the cuts, strokes, and general techniques used in relief woodcarving is to create a practice board. The example pictured was worked on an 11" x 14" x ¾" (279 x 356 x 19mm) basswood plaque. I used a ruler and pencil to mark a guideline grid of five squares by six squares, with most squares measuring 1½" (38mm).

The carving pictured was worked from one of the patterns available for the practice board (see page 55) and carved in a 15½" x 7½" x ¾" (394 x 191 x 19mm) butternut jewelry box lid.

As you create the practice board, each new technique will build on the steps you have already completed. As your skills grow, you can return to the board or create an entirely new one to experiment with new textures and cutting styles.

I use my practice board very often. For example, I used square eighteen to develop a wood grain background pattern I wanted to add to one of my carvings. By first working the pattern on my practice board, I was able to explore which tools and tool cuts created the best wood grain look before starting work on my main project.

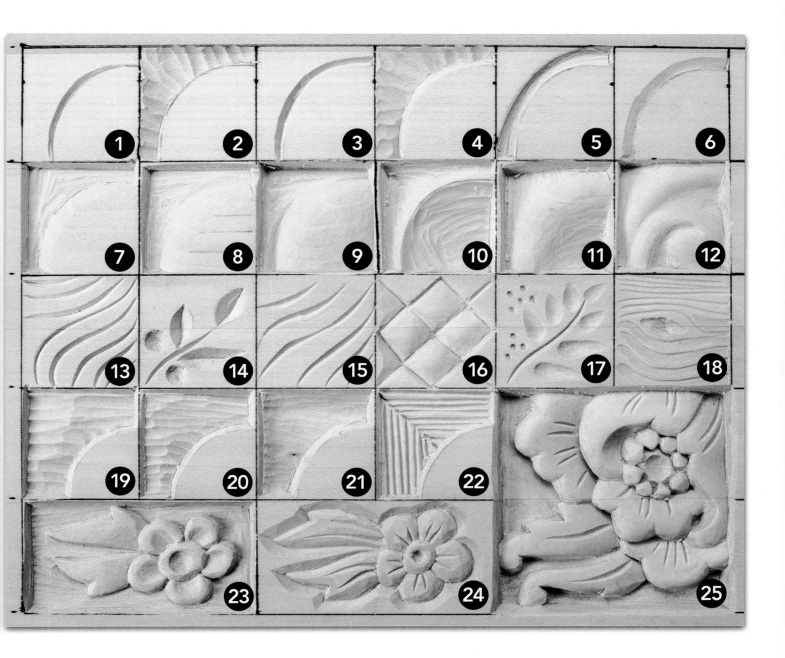

Each square of the guideline grid is used to carve one (or more) simple, basic technique:

- **Squares 1–6:** Basic element intersection treatments
- **Squares 7–12:** Basic edge and element shaping
- **Squares 13–18:** Traditional carving patterns
- **Squares 19–22:** Basic background treatments
- **Squares 23–25:** Practice designs

Square 1: Bench Knife Stop Cut

A stop cut separates two elements or areas within your pattern with a cut that stops the cutting stroke of a round gouge or chisel during the rough out stage or shaping stage. In this example, the stop cut is made using a bench knife, which creates a straight or 90°-angle wall along the higher element area.

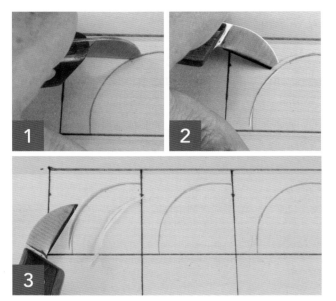

1 **Make the first cut.** Hold your bench knife in a comfortable writing position. Run the blade along the pattern line, making a shallow cut.

2 **Make the second cut.** Make a second cut with the bench knife, positioning it approximately ¹⁄₁₆" (2mm) away from the first cut. Angle your knife's tip into the first cut while making the second cut.

3 **Remove the wood.** This two-stroke cut removes a thin V-trough sliver of wood. As you work the background area, deepen the stop cut by reworking these two cuts.

Square 2: Bench Knife Stop Cut Rough Out

A stop cut is used to stop the cutting stroke of a round gouge or chisel as you drop the background element into the wood. Both round gouges and chisels are used to rough out and remove the excess background wood.

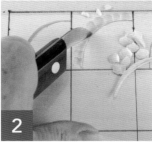

1 **Create a stop cut, and begin removing wood.** Following the steps employed for Square 1, create a stop cut along the pattern line using your bench knife. Using a medium to large round gouge or chisel, begin removing the excess wood in the background area, moving the gouge or chisel from the background element area into the stop cut.

2 **Continue removing wood, and free any chips.** Working along the pattern line, several gouge or chisel cuts can be made at a time. Bring the gouge or chisel directly against the stop cut. Free the gouge or chisel chips by re-cutting the stop cut with your bench knife. Do not break off these chips with your fingers. Broken chips can damage the stop cut edge of the element.

Square 3: V-Gouge Stop Cut

The V-gouge has a bent cutting blade to create a sharp, angled V-cut. Most beginner carving tool kits include a 90˚ V-gouge, but V-gouges are available in a variety of angles.

1 **Create the V-gouge stop cut.** A V-gouge cuts a stop cut in just one stroke. The angle at which you hold the tool determines the slant of the element walls. You can deepen a V-gouge stop cut by reworking the cut several times. Free the end of the V-cut with your bench knife.

Square 4: V-gouge Stop Cut Rough Out

The trough created by a V-gouge stops the cutting strokes from a round gouge or chisel during the rough out stage.

1 **Make a stop cut and rough out the background.** Create your stop cut using a V-gouge. Using a round gouge or chisel, work from the background element into the stop cut, removing the excess wood. Bring the gouge or chisel cut into the stop cut. Using a bench knife or V-gouge, rework the stop cut to free the background chips.

Square 5: Narrow Channel Rough Out

The corners of tight or narrow areas between elements in a relief carving are chip carved to remove a small triangular shape. The channel is then dropped to level using a veining tool.

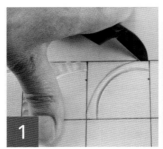
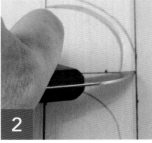

1 **Make the first chip cut.** Using your chip carving knife, make a straight cut into the wood along one pattern line by pushing the point into the corner.

2 **Make the second chip cut.** Make a second chip knife cut, working the point into the corner of the pattern lines on the second side of the chip area.

Square 5: continued

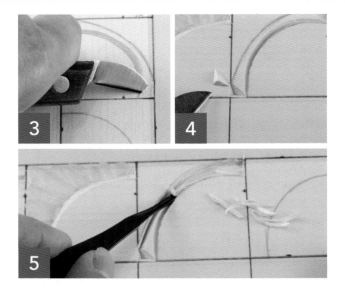

3 **Make the third chip cut.** Place your knife at a 45° angle to the wood. Make a cut from the end of the first chip cut to the end of the second chip cut.

4 **Remove the chip.** This simple three-cut process removes a neat, small triangle from the corner area of the design.

5 **Make any additional chip cuts and rough cut the channel.** After the four corners of the tight, narrow area have been removed by making chip cuts, use a tight U-gouge or veining tool to rough cut the channel.

Square 6: Straight Chisel Edges

The straight chisel and skew chisel can be used to create a beveled edge along a bench knife stop cut. This beveled edge separates the carved element from an uncarved background area.

Before you start cutting this square, you should know that straight chisels have one side of their cutting edge sharpened to a 12° to 20° bevel. The underside of the cutting edge is level or straight with the tool's shaft. If you hold a straight chisel with the flat side against the wood, the bevel side visible, the tool will take a thick, deep slice of wood. Reversing the tool's position with the flat side visible and the bevel side against the wood allows you to take extremely thin shavings along the wood's surface.

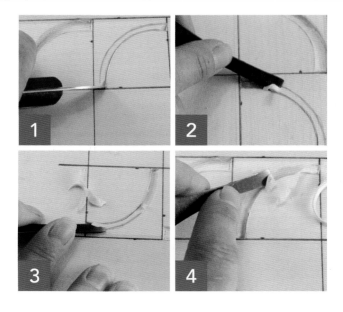

1 **Make a stop cut and chip cut the corners.** Using a bench knife, create a stop cut along the pattern line. Chip cut the corner points.

2 **Make the first chisel cut.** Using a straight chisel, glide the cutting edge along the outer edge of the stop cut, working the edge at the bevel angle you desire.

3 **Make any additional chisel cuts.** The background chisel bevel can be worked in several directions, joining the cuts at the center point of the bevel.

4 **Shave the bevel.** Shave the bevel cut by holding the chisel low to the cut with the flat side facing out. This removes very thin slivers of wood.

Square 7: Simple Rounded-Over Edge

The simplest method of dressing or shaping a relief element is to round over the edge. Rounding over is most often done using a straight chisel or skew chisel, but you may also use a bench knife, detail knife, or chip carving knife.

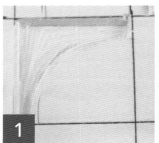

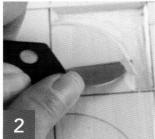

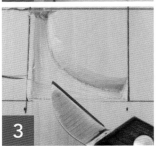

1 **Rough cut the background.** Rough cut the background area surrounding your element using a bench knife, V-gouge, and round gouge.

2 **Bevel the edge.** Using a straight chisel, skew chisel, or bench knife, cut along the edge of the element, holding the knife at a slight bevel. Several cuts may be needed to shape or roll over the edge. Turn the wood blank as necessary to work with the grain lines of the wood in the area being cut.

3 **Round over the edge.** Round over just the edge of the element, leaving the deeper walls of the element at a 90° angle to the background, or cut the edge from the background to the uncarved surface of the element into a quarter-circle shape.

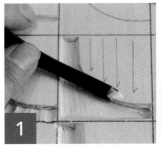

Square 8: Deep Rounded-Over Edge

To give more shape to an element than a simple rounded-over edge, you may wish to deeply round or roll the edge area. This rounding over technique uses a bench knife and a straight chisel and/or skew chisel.

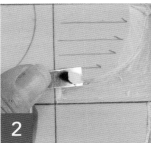

1 **Rough out the background.** Rough out the background area surrounding your element using your bench knife and round gouge.

2 **Round over the edge.** Using either the bench knife or straight chisel, shape the edge of the element into a deep rounded slope. The deeper the rounded-over edge, the farther you will need to cut into the element area. Notice in the photo how far toward the center point of the element the chisel cuts have been made. This gives a long sloping line from the element to the background area.

Square 8: continued

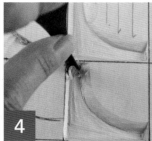

3 **Clean up the intersection.** After the wall edge of the element has been rounded, you may need to clean the intersection point of the element's edge with the background level.

4 **Cut along the intersection.** Using a V-gouge, cut along the joint line between the element and the background. Upend the V-gouge and gently push the tool's cutting edge into the corners to create crisp, clean walls. Any tool can be upended. V-gouges used in this manner create perfect right-angle cuts. A round gouge can be upended and rolled along the wood surface to cut a perfect circle. For very sharp, straight walls, upend your straight chisel.

Square 9: Convex Curves
For more complex relief carvings, you might want to shape more than just the edge of an element. In this example, the element—the quarter circle—has been worked so that the entire element surface forms a convex curve.

1 **Rough cut the background and round over the edge.** Rough cut the background area by making a stop cut using a bench knife and removing the excess wood with a medium or large round gouge. Using the bench knife or a straight chisel, roll the edge of the curved element into a deep round over. Continue rolling the element using your straight chisel, working the roll into the lower right-hand corner of the curve.

2 **Smooth the surface.** Rework the curved element using your straight chisel with the beveled cutting edge against the wood to shave the convex curve smooth.

Square 10: Concave Curves

While a convex curve is rounded outward like a ball, a concave curve drops into the wood like the inside of a bowl. In this example, both the background area and the quarter circle element are worked into concave curves.

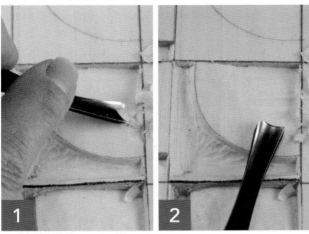

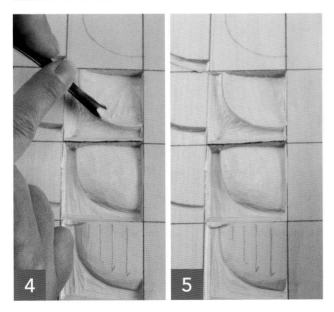

1 **Make stop cuts and begin shaping the elements.** Create bench knife stop cuts along the straight edges of the element. Using a medium or large round gouge, drop the lower right corner of the element. Work your gouge from the center of the element toward that corner.

2 **Refine the shape of the element.** Begin each gouge cut as a shallow cut. To create the concave curve shape, slowly deepen the cut as you near the lower right corner.

3 **Clean up the edges.** A V-gouge can be used to clean the round gouge cuts along the straight edges of the element.

4 **Shape the curved edge.** Roll your medium round gouge along the top, outer edge of the curved edge of the element to create a crisp, sharp angle between it and the background.

5 **Select a treatment for your project.** You can see all four element treatments in this photo. From bottom to top: simple rounded-over edge, deeply rounded-over edge, convex curve, and concave curve. Select the one you like the best or that best fits your project, and apply it to your relief carving.

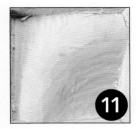

Square 11: Compound Curves

Curved areas that roll from concave to convex are called compound curves.

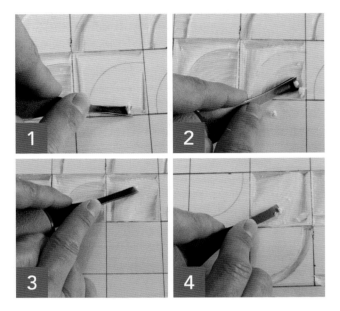

1 **Make stop cuts and drop the corners.** Cut along the outside edge of the pattern lines with a bench knife. Using a V-gouge, drop the level of the wood to the desired depth in the two opposing corners.

2 **Create a concave curve.** Using a round gouge, create a concave curve inside the quarter-circle area, tapering the curve from the quarter-circle pattern line to the lower right corner. Roll the area outside of the quarter-circle toward the upper right corner.

3 **Round over the edge.** Using a straight chisel, round over the high area of the compound curve along the quarter-circle pattern line.

4 **Smooth the curve.** Continue using the straight chisel to shave the compound curve smooth.

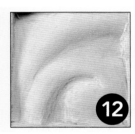

Square 12: Complex Curves and Shaving

Many of the curves found in relief carvings are complex, rolling from deep concaves up to multiple convex curves to create the final shape of an element.

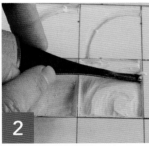

1 **Create the necessary stop cuts.** Using a V-gouge and bench knife, create any stop cuts needed along the pattern lines.

2 **Rough cut the curves.** Rough carve the curves of the pattern with your round gouges and straight chisel.

Square 12: continued

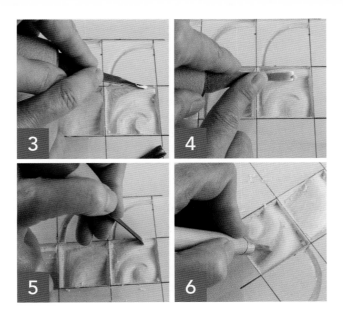

3 Carve the tight areas. Tight areas within the element can be rough carved using U-gouges and a veining gouge.

4 Begin smoothing the element. Begin smoothing the rough carved areas using a straight chisel. Turn the chisel to place the beveled cutting edge (front edge) of the tool against the wood. Hold the chisel at a low angle to the wood to cut away extremely thin slivers.

5 Finish smoothing the element. To remove any remaining gouge ridges, upend your straight chisel and pull the cutting edge across the surface to be smoothed.

6 Give the concave curves a final smoothing. Upend a round gouge to give the concave curves a final smoothing. Pull the gouge so that the back side rubs along the curves.

Square 13: Free-Form Stop Cuts

Very fine line work can be created using stop cuts made with chip carving or bench knives.

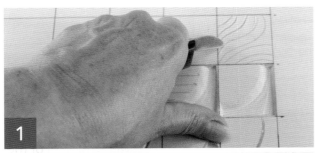

1 Create two-stroke stop cuts. Two-stroke stop cuts, made with either a bench knife or chip carving knife, can be used to create fine line designs within your pattern.

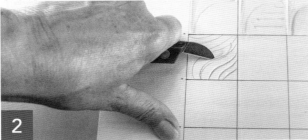

2 Angle your knife to create a V-shaped trough. By angling the chip knife away from the pattern line as you make both sides of the cut, you create a fine V-trough center. By keeping the knife's tip high in the wood at the beginning and end of the stop cut and deeper near the center of the cut, the finished line varies from thin to thick to thin.

Square 14: Free-Form Chip Carving and Upending

Free-form chip cuts, created on their own or paired with free-form stop cuts, can add detail to a relief carving project. You can create additional detail by using a round gouge to make circle indents in the wood.

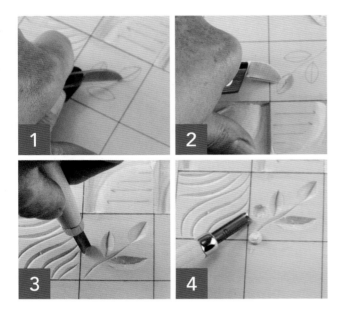

1 **Cut the centerline of the leaf pattern.** Create wide free-form chips with a chip carving knife. To create the leaves shown, cut along the centerline of the leaf pattern to separate the two sides of the leaf. Then, place the tip of your knife to the side of one tip of the leaf.

2 **Cut the outer pattern lines.** As you pull the knife along the outer pattern line, roll the knife angle away from the leaf area. Make the cut shallow at the leaf point, deeper at the center, and then return to the shallow depth at the opposite point.

3 **Begin creating the circular indents.** By upending your round gouge, you can cut perfect small round indents like the ones at the base of this leaf pattern. Hold the gouge upright against the wood on its cutting edge. Gently roll the gouge in your fingers to cut a fine line, creating the outline of your circle.

4 **Finish the circular indents.** Continue rolling the gouge to deepen the cut as you slowly drop the angle of the gouge away from the circle area. As you drop and roll the gouge, the tool will cut to the center of the concave circle, releasing a small circular chip of wood.

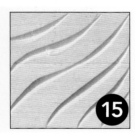

Square 15: V-Gouge Free-Form Stop Cuts

The V-gouge can be used to create free-form stop cut lines.

1 **Create the free-form stop cuts.** A V-gouge cuts both sides of a free-form line with just one cutting stroke. Begin with the cutting tip of the gouge high in the wood. As you move the V-gouge through the stroke, deepen the tip into the cut to create deeper and wider areas in your line. As you near the end of the free-form line, bring the V-gouge back to a shallow depth.

Square 16: Background Pillows

Small square or rectangular convex pillows are a long-standing, traditional background fill pattern.

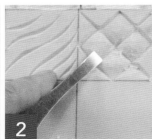

1 **Create grid lines, and cut along each one with a V-gouge.** With a pencil and ruler, create a grid pattern of squares in your background area. The squares in this example are arranged diagonally to the board. Using a V-gouge, cut along the pencil grid lines to separate the squares.

2 **Make each square convex.** Use a straight chisel to roll each square into a convex form. Shave each square smooth. Recut the square's separation lines with the V-gouge if needed.

Square 17: Round Gouge Spoon Carving

Using just a round gouge, you can create a traditional carving style called spoon carving, which was extremely popular during the Victorian era. Spoon carving elements were often used to decorate drawer fronts, candle shelves, and spoon racks.

1 **Cut a leaf shape.** A simple leaf shape can be made using your round gouge. Holding the gouge at a low angle to the wood, begin your cut at the wide base of the leaf and bring the gouge down into the wood for the deepest point in the stroke. As you move the gouge through the leaf, slowly raise the gouge in depth until you end the leaf with a fine, shallow point.

2 **Add detail as desired.** For this example, small round indents were created using a small U-gouge to accent the leaves. A free-form stop cut line finishes the example.

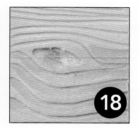

Square 18: Wood Grain Texture

Wood grain is a favorite background pattern that is easy to create using your V-gouge, straight chisel, and round gouge.

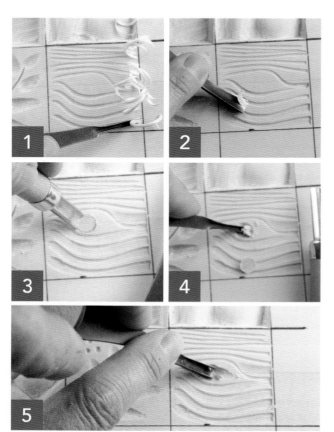

1 **Make cuts along the wood grain.** Whenever possible, work the wood grain texture pattern with the wood grain of your carving blank. Begin by cutting along each grain line using a tight U-gouge or veining tool.

2 **Bevel the edges of the cuts.** Using either your large round gouge or straight chisel, bevel the side of each grain line on the inside (the knothole side) of the line. Vary the width and depth of the bevels.

3 **Create a large knothole.** Upend a large or medium round gouge to create the large knothole of the pattern.

4 **Create an inner knothole.** Use a small round gouge or a small U-gouge to create a smaller, inside knothole.

5 **Refine the edges of the knothole.** Using a medium round gouge or medium U-gouge, cut a spoon carving shape along both sides of the knothole.

Square 19: Rough Round Gouge Background Texture

You can use your early rough out stage round gouge strokes to create a wide, thick texture in the background of your carving.

1 **Create and refine several rough out cuts.** The early rough out cuts made with your large round gouge or large U-gouge can become a deeply textured background. After the design carving has been completed, use your bench knife and V-gouge to clean the join lines between the background and the design. Remove any small, round gouge chips from the background, and then give the background a light sanding using 220-grit sandpaper.

Square 20: Small Round Gouge Background Texture

To add to the interest of a round gouge textured background, you can use gouges of several different sizes to create varied gouge strokes.

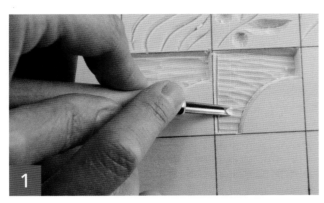

1 **Rough out the background area with a large gouge, and then refine with a smaller gouge.** After you have roughed out your background area with a large round gouge, you can add more texture strokes by recutting some areas using a medium or small round gouge. Smaller gouge cuts will fill the background with more gouge ridges. In this sample, the background area of the practice square has been tapered from the outer boundaries of the square into the pattern area. Tapering allows you to move smoothly from a high outer border to the depth needed for your design's background level.

Square 21: Smooth Tapered Background

Smoothing the background that surrounds your carved designs diminishes the importance of that area, bringing more attention to your design elements.

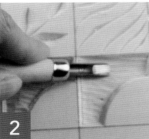

1 **Select the best background for your design.** Texture attracts attention. When you want the viewer's focus to fall solely on the carved design of your project, reduce the amount of texture in the background areas.

2 **Smooth any rough cut background areas.** To work this tapered, smooth background, recut the background several times using a wide round gouge or a wide sweep gouge. Finish the area by shaving away any small ridges that remain.

Square 22: Patterned Background

The background area of your carving board can be incorporated into the design area by using a repeating pattern.

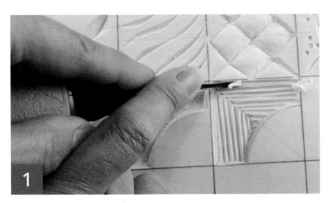

1 **Select and carve a pattern.** The simple straight-line pattern shown was cut with a small U-gouge. It adds a repeating line design to the background of the carving. To create this pattern, mark the diagonal centerline of the square with a pencil. Mark several guidelines on either side of the diagonal that move outward from the diagonal, parallel to the boundary edges of the square. Working from the diagonal line and following the guidelines, cut a series of parallel lines with a small U-gouge.

Square 23: Practice Carving 1

This super simple flower pattern will allow you to apply many of the basic techniques previously learned in this chapter.

1 **Trace the pattern.** Trace a pattern (see page 55) to your practice board using graphite paper.

2 **Create the necessary stop and chip cuts.** Create bench knife stop cuts along the outer edges of the pattern. Cut triangular chip cuts in the background corners of the petals.

Square 23: continued

3 Rough cut the background. Working with the grain of the wood, rough cut the background area using a medium round gouge.

4 Cut the background level to the proper depth. Rough cut the background to a depth of ³⁄₁₆" (5mm), making straight outer walls along your design elements.

5 Make stop cuts between the leaves and petals. Using your V-gouge, create stop cuts between the leaf elements and the flower petals in the design.

6 Taper the leaves into convex curves. Using a straight chisel, taper the base of each leaf into the flower petals. Taper the outer leaf points away from the flower. This forms the leaves into convex curves.

7 Taper the leaf edges. Taper the long sides of the leaves toward the background area using your straight chisel.

8 Stop cut around the center circle. Using a V-gouge, make a stop cut along the line for the center circle of the flower.

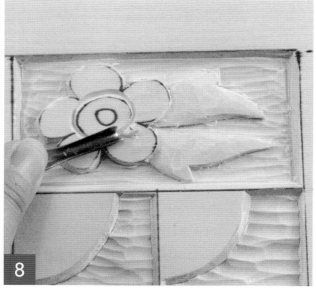

Square 23: continued

9 **Give each petal a concave shape.** Using a medium round gouge or a medium U-gouge, create a concave indent inside each flower petal.

10 **Separate the flower petals.** Separate each flower petal using a V-gouge and a stop cut.

11 **Cut the flower's inner circle.** Upend a medium or large round gouge to cut the inner circle of the flower's center.

12 **Round over the petal edges.** Using a straight chisel, round over the outer edges of each flower petal.

13 **Clean up the design elements.** Smooth the carving by shaving each element—leaves, petals, and flower center. Recut the intersection/joint lines between the elements and the background.

14 **Finish cleaning up the design and sand.** After a few more cleaning cuts and a touch of sanding using 220-grit sandpaper, this carving is complete and ready to be painted or finished.

Square 24: Practice Carving 2

This simple practice carving uses a tight beveled edge to surround the design, separating it from the uncarved background area of the board.

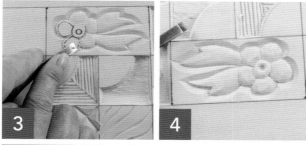

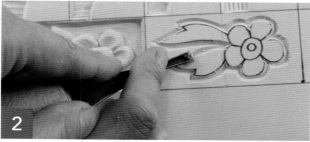

1 **Trace the pattern.** Transfer a pattern (see page 55) to your practice board using graphite paper.

2 **Create stop cuts along the pattern outline.** Using a V-gouge, stop cut along the outside pattern lines. Hold the V-gouge so that both sides of the cut are evenly angled from the center of the pattern line.

3 **Shape the design element.** Round over, shape, and add detail to the flower and leaves following Steps 5–12 in Square 23, Practice Carving 1.

4 **Check your progress.** When you have finished shaping the flower and leaves, the V-gouge stop cut should form a separation line between the carved design area and the uncarved background of the board.

5 **Add some detail.** Add a few V-gouge free-form strokes as leaf veins and petal folds to the design. Then, give the carving a final smoothing and a light sanding using 220-grit sandpaper.

Square 25: Practice Carving 3

Stylized flowers are a traditional pattern style used to accent furniture, jewelry boxes, and wall plaques. This detailed carving uses an undercutting technique to add extra dark shadows to the finished work.

1 Trace the pattern. Transfer a pattern (see page 55) to your practice board using graphite paper.

2 Stop cut along the outline and rough cut the background. Stop cut along the outer pattern lines using a bench knife. Then, rough cut the background area using a round gouge.

3 Clean up the edges. Clean and straighten the outer walls of the design area using a straight chisel.

4 Make a depth gauge. You can create a simple depth gauge by cutting a piece of chipboard. Place the chipboard down into your carving and mark the carved depth on the gauge with a pencil. You can now move the gauge to the next carving area to compare the depth of your work and ensure that it is even.

5 Number the elements and shape the leaves. Number each design element according to the element's height in the carving. I chose to label the background area of this carving as 1 and the highest elements as 4. Round and shape the leaves using a straight chisel.

6 Cut and shape the outer petals. Stop cut the outer petals using a bench knife. Using a round gouge, carve the petals into a concave shape, with the deepest point of the curve against the flower's center.

Square 25: continued

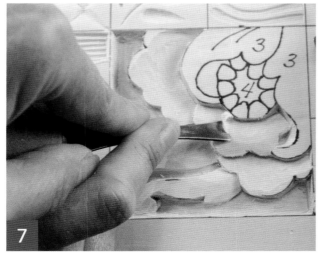

7 **Cut and shape the lower center petal.** Stop cut the lower center petal with a bench knife. Carve this petal into a convex curve using a round gouge and straight chisel.

8 **Check your progress and carving depth.** Alternating concave and convex curves throughout the petals of the flower gives the flower a greater impression of realism. Note that the inner edges of all three petals carved so far should be worked as deeply into the wood as the roughed out background areas. Use your depth gauge to check your progress.

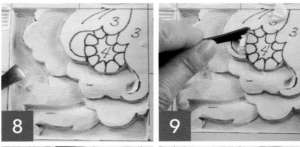

9 **Cut and shape the area next to the upper center petal.** Stop cut the area captured between the upper center petal and the flower's center. Using a round gouge, curve this area into the flower's center.

10 **Cut and shape the right petal.** Stop cut along the edge of the outer right flower petal using a bench knife. With your round gouge or straight chisel, curve this petal from the high point at the flower's center to the depth of the rough cut background at the corner of the square.

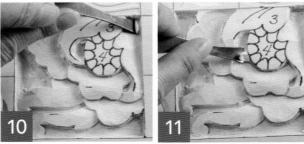

11 **Work the inner edge of the upper petal.** Roll over the inner edge of the upper center petal using a round gouge.

12 **Work the outer edge of the upper petal.** Roll the outer area of the upper center petal into a convex curve, with the deepest area of the curve at the outer edge along the edge of the square.

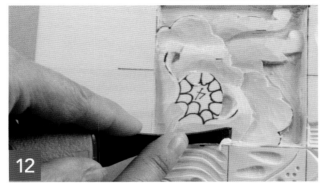

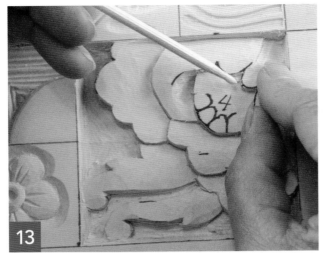

13 **Be prepared for mistakes.** Mistakes happen! In this photo I stop cut the flower center where it touches the upper center petal and outer right petal using a bench knife. During the cutting process, I broke a small area of the outer right petal's edge.

14 **Repair any mistakes.** Small breaks and chips can be repaired with a small amount of wood glue. Apply a drop of glue under the chipped area and then press the chip back into position. Allow about fifteen minutes for the glue to dry before you continue carving in that area.

15 **Round the flower's center.** Using a round gouge, round the entire center of the flower into an even convex curve.

16 **Mark the flower's center.** With a pencil, re-mark the center circle of the flower's center. Divide the center area into eight even sections.

17 **Cut an indentation in the flower's center.** Use a medium round gouge to cut the inner part of the flower's center into a concave bowl shape.

18 **Stop cut along the centerlines.** Using a bench knife, create stop cuts along each of the center section lines.

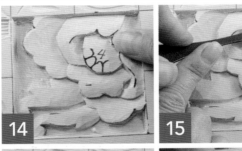

Square 25: continued

19 **Check your progress.** With Step 18 complete, the basic shaping steps are finished.

20 **Smooth the background and petals.** Return to the background and smooth the gouge lines by upending a chisel or round gouge to shave away the fine ridges. When you have finished smoothing the background, shave the petals smooth.

21 **Round over the petal edges.** Using a straight chisel, round over the edges of all the flower petals.

22 **Continue refining the design.** Wherever necessary, recut or reshape the design elements to create smooth curves and even transitions.

23 **Round the center petals.** Using a bench knife, lightly round over the small petals that surround the flower's center.

24 **Begin making undercuts.** You can create a deep shadow in a design by tucking the joint line of two elements under the edge of the higher element. An undercut is made using two cutting strokes. First, cut just above the joint line between the two elements with a bench knife held at a low angle and pointed into the higher element. Make several light cuts to slowly push the knife's tip deep under the higher element.

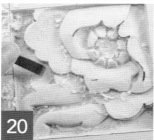

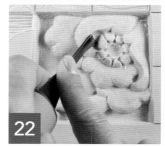

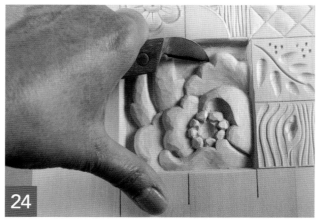

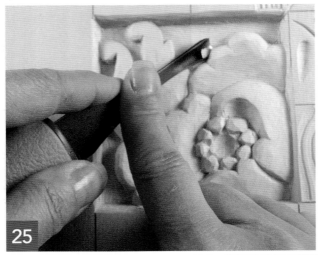

25 **Make the second undercut cutting stroke.** The second cut of an undercut removes a small sliver of wood, tucking the joint line between the elements under the higher element. You will make the second cut with a wide sweep gouge, large round gouge, or dogleg chisel. Hold this tool so the cutting edge is as level as possible with the lower element. Cut along the joint line between the elements, working the tool's edge into the first bench knife cut.

26 **Create an undercut along the upper petal.** Work an undercut along the left edge of the upper center petal between the upper center petal and lower center petal.

27 **Check your progress.** The completed undercut should create shadows in the design, as seen in this photo.

28 **Add some free-form cuts and finish the design.** Complete the carving by adding a few free-form stop cuts with a bench knife to add folds to the flower petals and veins to the leaves. The design is then ready for a final cleanup and light sanding using 220-grit sandpaper.

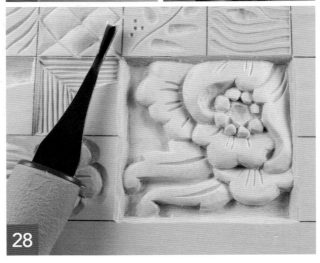

Flower pattern options

Patterns shown at 100% for practice board.

This pattern can be used for larger relief carving projects, such as the jewelry box lid shown on page 32. If desired, it can also be reduced by 50% and used for Square 25 of the practice board.

PRACTICE PROJECT:
Birch Bark Swan

Sgraffito

Russian birch bark carving uses little or no shaping of the individual elements of a pattern. Instead, the entire design is created through fine line work done with the bench knife, chip carving knife, and V-gouge. A small round gouge is used to create a few teardrop-shaped strokes in the large areas of the pattern. Its simplicity makes the birch bark carving technique an excellent pattern for a first carving.

In this folk art style of carving, a thin veneer of birch is glued to a darker wood board, such as black walnut or mahogany. The design is developed by cutting thin strips from the pale white birch to expose the dark wood below. For this practice project, you will apply this carving technique to a basswood plaque.

Tools and Supplies

- 11" x 14" x ¾" (279 x 356 x 19mm) basswood plaque
- Graphite tracing paper
- Painter's tape
- Pencil
- Bench knife
- Chip carving knife

- V-gouge
- Tight U-gouge
- Small round gouge
- Sharpening tools and strop
- 220-grit sandpaper
- Soft, clean cloth

- Stiff toothbrush or dusting brush
- Paintbrush
- Sanding sealer
- Pecan oil stain
- Polyurethane spray sealer
- Thick terrycloth towel or nonslip mat

1 **Prepare the carving blank.** Begin your practice carving by preparing the basswood plaque. Using 220-grit sandpaper, smooth the carving surface and edges of the plaque. Remove any dust with a clean, soft cloth.

2 **Trace the pattern.** Using graphite paper, trace the pattern to the basswood plaque.

3 **Cut along the pattern lines.** Using a bench knife and/or chip carving knife, cut a thin line along each of the pattern tracing lines.

4 **Lower the background.** Use a small round gouge to lower the background area outside the center circle to about ¹⁄₁₆"–⅛" (2–3mm) deep. Work these strokes with the grain of the wood plaque.

5 **Carve the circle background.** Using a tight U-gouge, carve the background area behind the swan scene inside of the circle. Keep the cuts tightly packed and worked with the grain of the wood.

6 **Carve the feather details.** Add fine curved feather lines using a V-gouge in the tail and underbelly area of the swan.

7 **Define the water and large feathers.** Use the small round gouge to establish the water. Make a teardrop-shaped cut using a round gouge in the center of each of the large feathers.

8 **Add any fine details desired.** Fine detailing lines can be cut using a bench knife, U-gouge (top), small round gouge (middle), and V-gouge (bottom).

9 **Clean up the carving.** Clean the carving with a stiff toothbrush or dusting brush to remove stray or loose wood fibers. If necessary, lightly sand any rough areas of the project. Clean away the sanding dust with a soft cloth.

10 **Apply sanding sealer.** Following the manufacturer's instructions, brush two coats of sanding sealer on the top and edges of the carving. Allow each coat to dry thoroughly, and lightly sand between coats using 220-grit sandpaper.

11 **Apply spray sealer.** Apply one to two coats of polyurethane spray sealer to the carving, following the directions on the label. Allow the carving to dry.

12 **Stain the carving.** Apply one coat of pecan oil stain to the carving and wipe immediately with a soft cotton cloth. Because basswood stains quickly, work in small 3"–5" (76–127mm)-square sections at a time. Allow the carving to dry.

13 **Finish the carving.** Finish the carving with one to two coats of polyurethane spray sealer.

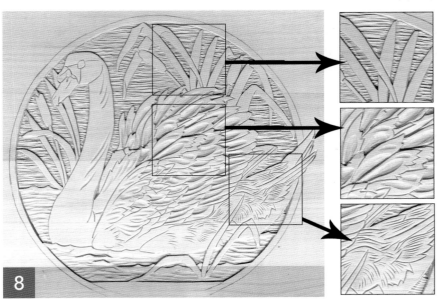

LEVEL	DEPTH
1	Surface
2	1/16"–1/8" (2–3mm)
B	Background 1/16"–1/8" (2–3mm)

Pattern shown at 100%.

A

Note: This pattern contains rough estimates of the depth measurements for each level based on the thickness of the board I used to carve this project. Remember that relief carvings should generally be worked in the top half of your wood blank. Adjust these measurements as necessary according to the thickness of the blank you're using.

A

PROJECT:
Country Goose Barn

General Relief Carving Review Low Relief

This small carving has eight distinct levels of work. Working from the background of the pattern to the foreground they are: level 8 sky shown in dark brown, level 7 background trees shown in medium brown, level 6 silo in brown, level 5 barn in light brown, level 4 the deep mid-ground grass in dark tan, level 3 the mid-ground grass in medium tan, level 2 the goose in tan, and level 1 the foreground grass in light tan.

Tools and Supplies

- 9" x 12" x ¾" (229 x 305 x 19mm) basswood plaque
- V-gouge
- Small and large round gouges
- Wide sweep round gouge
- Straight chisel
- Bull-nose chisel
- Tight U-gouge

- Bench knife or chip carving knife
- Sharpening tools and strop
- Sandpaper, 220- and 320-grit
- Graphite tracing paper
- Painter's tape
- Pencil
- Soft, clean cloth

- Dusting brush
- Transparent tape
- Sanding sealer
- Brush-on or spray polyurethane sealer
- Fine-point permanent marker
- Thick terrycloth towel or nonslip mat

General Relief Carving Review

Before you begin carving this project, it is important to remember that every relief carving goes through several stages:

1. The pattern is worked to reduce the design to layers or groups of elements, called a simplified pattern. The pattern is also adjusted in size to fit your carving blank.

2. The simplified pattern is traced to the wood with all borders, margins, or added hardware areas noted in pencil.

3. The background area is rough cut to drop it to the lowest level in the design.

4. The rough cut or rough out of each level is worked. By carving a large grouping of elements at one time, you can drop all the elements into the wood easily. Each layer or level is rough cut to its general depth in the wood.

5. The layers of the carving are put through a smoothing process. This allows you to retrace any small elements into their respective layers.

6. Each small layer unit or element unit is carved to add even more dimension to the work.

7. A second retracing establishes the detail lines for the project. These lines are cut using a V-gouge or a two-step stop cut with the bench knife.

8. The project receives its final smoothing, and then the painting and finishing steps are completed.

In the case of this project, the carving process starts by establishing the levels through the roughing out process using a round gouge, V-gouge, and bench knife. Then, each area receives some simple shaping. The carving is then dressed out using shaving and sanding to smooth the surface in preparation for retracing the pattern lines onto each area to add in detail lines.

The details are cut into each area using a V-gouge, U-gouge, and small round chisel. To complete the project, I used craft paints to add a bright country finish.

Depth gauges

The depth gauge for this project and all others throughout this book contain rough estimates and not exact measurements. During the early rough out stage of carving, your levels will vary greatly in depth because of the natural ridges left by the round gouge.

I will often leave my levels in the rough out stage slightly proud—higher than the final desired depth. Each level will drop slightly in depth during the smoothing steps and detail cutting. For example, when this carving was complete, I measured the far background at ⅝" (16mm) deep at its deepest point. During the rough out stage, I only dropped the background to about ½" (13mm) deep. The remaining ⅛" (3mm) of wood was removed during the smoothing and final detailing and texturing steps that were worked later in the carving process.

LEVEL	DEPTH
1	Surface
2	1/16" (2mm)
3	1/8" (3mm)
4	1/4" (6mm)
5	5/16" (8mm)
6	3/8" (10mm)
7	7/16" (11mm)
8	5/8" (16mm)

Simple pattern. In this simple pattern of the *Country Goose Barn* there are eight main elements of the design, each of which can become one level within the design.

Enlarge Pattern 110%

Note: This pattern contains rough estimates of the depth measurements for each level based on the thickness of the board I used to carve this project. Remember that relief carvings should generally be worked in the top half of your wood blank. Adjust these measurements as necessary according to the thickness of the blank you're using.

1 Prepare the carving blank and trace the pattern.
Prepare the basswood plaque by sanding the surface with 220-grit sandpaper. Remove the sanding dust with a clean, dry cloth. Make a copy of the pattern, center the pattern to the board, tape it in place, and use graphite paper to trace the outline of each of the elements.

2 Cut along the barn roof and background tree.
Using a V-gouge and/or bench knife, stop cut along the top tracing line of the barn roof and background tree.

3 Rough out the sky. Working level 8, use a round gouge and/or straight chisel to begin roughing out the sky area of the design. Work your cutting strokes from the top edge of the pattern into the stop cuts you made along the top line of the barn roof and background tree. As you work this area, the sky will develop a curve, the highest point of the curve at the top edge of the pattern and the lowest point at the barn roof and tree line.

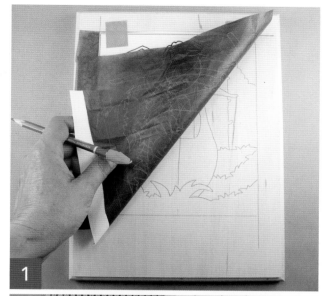

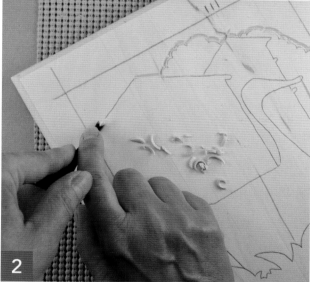

Removing Wood Fibers

Basswood and butternut are excellent woods for beginner carvers, as they are both very easy to cut compared to other common carving woods. This also means that more loose wood fibers are created during the carving process than with other woods. To remove these fibers I use sandpaper, foam core sanding boards, sanding pads, and a stiff brush. This extra sanding may not be necessary on woods that are harder than basswood and butternut.

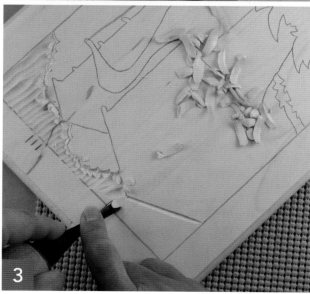

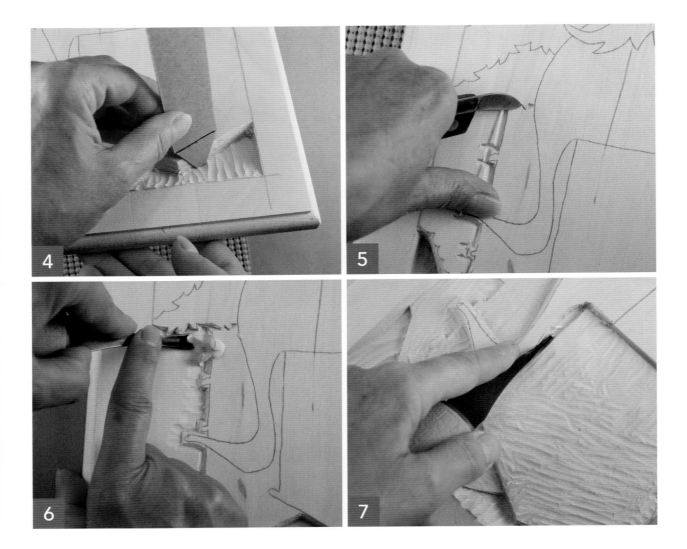

4 **Create a depth gauge for the sky level (level 8).** The sky area is the deepest point in this carving—just a little more than half the total thickness of the carving blank. Cut and mark a depth gauge for the sky area to ensure you do not cut more than ⅝" (16mm) deep.

5 **Begin shaping the background trees.** Begin work on the background trees (level 7). Use a V-gouge to make a stop cut along the right side of the silo. Then, use a bench knife or chip carving knife to make triangular chip cuts at the sharp corners of the pattern lines, such as the places where the tree branches meet.

6 **Cut the background tree to depth.** Using the round gouges or a straight chisel, rough cut the background tree down to its predetermined depth. Create and use a depth gauge to check your progress. Work the cutting strokes from the tree area toward the stop cuts along the silo and barn roof.

7 **Cut the silo and barn to depth.** Lower the silo (level 6) and barn (level 5) to depth in the same manner that you lowered the background trees in Step 6. The small portion of the silo behind the goose's neck can be cut using a tight U-gouge, or you can cut it using free-form chip cuts made with a bench knife or chip carving knife.

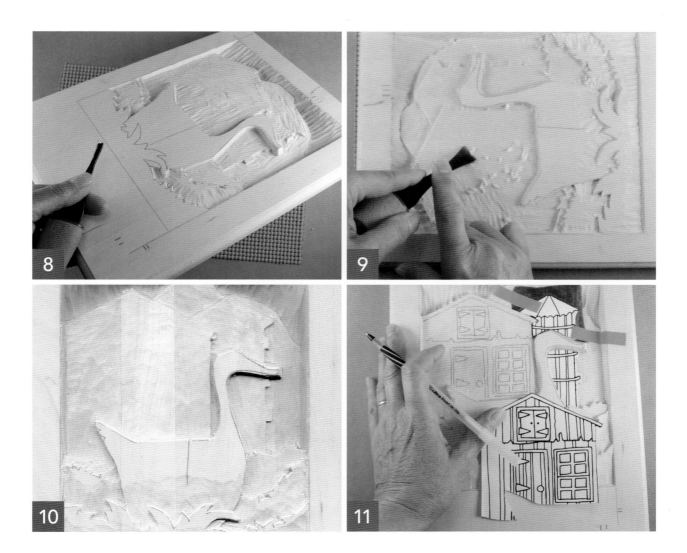

8 **Cut the grass to depth.** Lower the two grass areas (levels 5 and 4) located behind the goose in the same manner. The goose (level 2) and foreground grass (level 1) remain unworked at this stage.

9 **Smooth the entire carving.** With each element dropped to its appropriate depth, give the carving an overall general smoothing to prepare for retracing the pattern. A wide sweep round gouge, large round gouge, or bull-nose chisel can be used to remove the high ridges left from the rough out process.

10 **Check your progress.** At this stage, your carving should have distinct levels and a generally smoothed surface.

11 **Retrace the details.** Make a copy of the pattern and cut the pattern into pieces— one piece for each level in the design. Place and tape each pattern piece to its area of the carving. Using a small piece of graphite paper, trace the detail lines from the pattern to the board for each area of the pattern.

12 Begin shaping the barn. Begin a general shaping to each area of the pattern. Start with the barn by using a V-gouge to make a stop cut along the bottom edge of the roof line, and then lower the barn wall below the roof line with a round gouge. Using a V-gouge, make a stop cut along the barn's upper wall overhang line and along the outer lines of the door and window. Drop the lower barn wall slightly using a large round gouge or straight chisel.

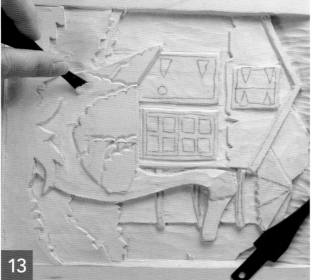

13 Cut and begin shaping the goose. Create stop cuts along the outlines of the goose pattern using a V-gouge. Using a wide sweep round gouge or large round gouge, taper each area toward the V-gouge stop cuts to give the goose some general shaping.

14 Shape and add texture to the background trees and silo. The top edge of the background trees contains small V-cuts that can be made by cutting small chip carved triangles from the wood with your bench knife, or by upending a V-gouge to make a V-cut and then releasing the V-gouge chip with a bench knife. Work a simple texture on the background trees by using a V-gouge to make groupings of shallow line cuts. Then, using a V-gouge, cut along the outlines of the three horizontal bands on the silo and the bottom edge of the silo roof. Lower the silo's form slightly below the level of the bands. Use a V-gouge to create a shallow wood texture. Texture the silo's metal roof with shallow small round gouge cuts.

15 Add texture and detail to the barn. Cut V-gouge troughs along the detail lines of the barn's windows and doors. Texture the barn doors using shallow V-gouge cuts. To create the windowpanes, upend your V-gouge and make a profile cut into each corner of every windowpane. Using your small round gouge, drop the panes slightly in depth. Upend a large round gouge to create the barn's doorknob.

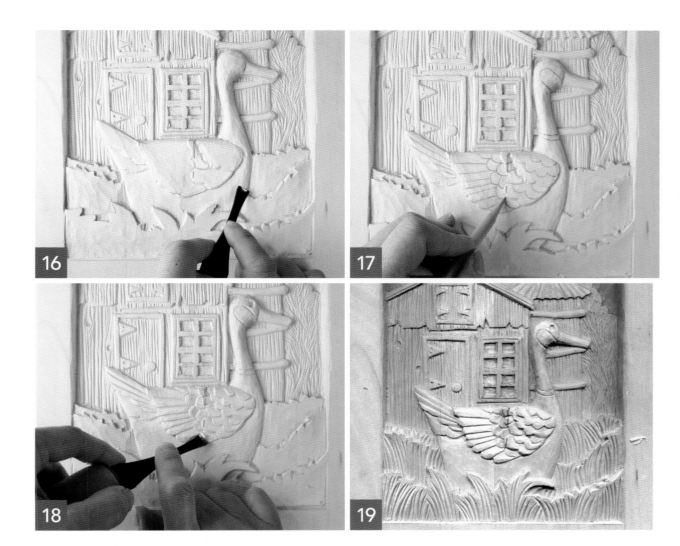

16 **Round the edges of the goose.** Using a straight chisel or a wide sweep round gouge, round over the edges of the each area of the goose. Cut along both sides of the goose's neck to roll this area. Use a V-gouge to cut a shallow trough separating the beak from the head.

17 **Retrace and cut the goose details.** As you work any relief project, you will need to retrace any detail pattern lines as needed. For the goose in this carving, retrace the pattern or use a soft #2 pencil to draw in the individual feather lines, neck band, and head band. Using a V-gouge, stop cut along each feather line and the head and neck bands.

18 **Shape the individual feathers.** Use a straight chisel or bull-nose chisel to taper each feather on the goose into the next overlapping feather. Upend a small round gouge to cut the outline of a small circle for the eye. Using a bench knife, remove the round gouge circle chip to create the indent for the eye.

19 **Add detail and texture to the grass.** Make V-cuts along the top edge of each of the grass areas by upending a V-gouge to make the cuts, and then releasing the chips with a bench knife. Add medium-deep V-gouge cuts throughout the grass areas to create the impression of individual blades of grass.

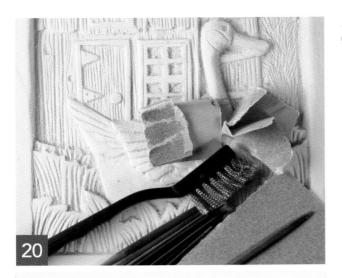

20

Reviewing Your Project

When Step 20 is complete, it is an excellent time to check your carving for any small areas that need attention. Here are some things you can look for:

1. Look for double V-gouge lines.
2. Recut wobbly V-gouge lines.
3. Check for even, smooth tapering from one area into the next, particularly at the joint lines between levels.
4. Look for any chipped areas where you may need to recut.
5. Search for any rough edges in rolled or rounded areas.
6. Check the intersections of carving strokes where one V-gouge line intersects another.

21

20 Smooth and sand the carving. Smooth each area of the carving by removing fine shavings with a straight chisel or a wide sweep gouge. After smoothing, very soft woods like basswood often need a light sanding to give each element an even surface and to remove any small wood fibers left behind after shaving and shaping. Sanding is done by working the entire carving with increasingly fine grits of sandpaper, beginning with 220-grit paper and finishing with 320-grit paper. Sandpaper grits are graded by the number of grit particles per inch—so a low grit number means there are fewer grit particles on the paper than paper with a higher grit number. Whenever possible, work sandpaper with the grain of the wood. Sanding lines can show up on a carving after a polyurethane or oil finish is applied, so avoid using a swirling or circular motion as you work the sandpaper. Remove sanding dust using a dusting brush, canned compressed air, or a lint-free tack cloth. Hardwoods like soft maple or mahogany may not require sanding, as they have a harder, denser, and sometimes more oily composition that results in cleaner cuts with fewer wood fibers left behind. Following the manufacturer's instructions, apply one coat of sanding sealer to the carving. Allow the sealer to dry well—at least one hour. Using 220- to 320-grit sandpaper, lightly sand the carving to remove any remaining wood fibers. Afterward, wipe the carving well with a dry cloth. Add another sanding sealer coating if necessary.

21 Select and apply a finishing treatment. At this stage, your carving is complete and is ready for the finishing steps. If you want to leave the carving as natural wood, you can apply two coats of brush-on polyurethane sealer, following the manufacturer's instructions. Spray-on polyurethane sealer is also an excellent choice for the sealer coating on a carving. If you wish to add color to your carving, apply one more very thin coat of sanding sealer and allow to dry overnight. See the next section for painting instructions.

22 Sign your carving. Turn your carving to the back. Using a fine-point permanent marker, sign and date the carving. If you plan on painting your carving, complete this step after all painting is complete and the paint has dried. Use two light coats of polyurethane spray sealer to give your painted carving the finishing coats it needs.

Painting your project

I chose to add color to my carving using acrylic craft paints. To paint your project as I did, start by placing a small amount of each paint color on a clean tile or on palette paper. Thin the colors by mixing equal parts paint and water together. Test the thinned mixtures by painting a small brush stroke on a sheet of newspaper. You should be able to see the paint's color while still being able to read the print underneath.

Apply one thinned coating of burnt umber or raw umber to the entire carved area of the wood. This will lightly antique the carved detail lines of the work. Allow the paint to dry for a few minutes.

Apply one coat of medium blue to the background sky. Brush a second coat of medium blue along the joint lines between the sky and the barn roof and background tree in the sky area.

Apply a thin coating of light verde green to the background tree. Then, accent this area with a few brushstrokes of cadmium yellow along the top edge of the treetop and medium verde green along the edge of the silo.

Add one to two coats of burnt umber to the barn roof. Use cadmium red for the barn walls, accented with a few brushstrokes of burnt umber under the roof's overhang and the top wall overhang. Trim the barn window and doors with titanium white. Use Payne's gray and carbon black for the windowpanes, door hinges, and doorknob, and for the front section of the goose's wing.

Paint the belly area of the goose with a very thin mixture of burnt umber and water. Use burnt umber for the long feathers of the wing. Apply two coats of carbon black for the head and tail. Fill the bottom of the tail, the neck band, and the head band with titanium white. Pick up a small bit of titanium white on a pencil point. Touch the pencil point to the eye to leave a small eye highlight dot.

Paint the foreground grass using light verde green, medium verde green, and cadmium yellow mixed half-and-half with titanium white.

Allow the colors to dry well overnight. Remember to sign your work and apply two additional coats of polyurethane spray sealer when the paint has dried, as described in Step 22.

Painting Supplies

■ Acrylic craft paints in:
- Burnt Umber or Raw Umber
- Medium Blue
- Light Verde Green
- Medium Verde Green
- Cadmium Yellow
- Cadmium Red
- Titanium White
- Payne's Gray
- Carbon Black

■ Assorted soft-bristle paintbrushes
■ Paper towels
■ Water
■ Glass tile, palette paper, or tinfoil

Painting Basswood

Basswood is not only a soft wood for carving, it is also very absorbent. Whether you are using acrylic paints, oil paints, or watercolors, raw basswood grabs color quickly. To slow or deter this tendency, apply a light coating of sealer—either sanding sealer or polyurethane spray sealer—to a basswood carving before painting.

PROJECT:
Mayan High Priest

Low Relief

The *Mayan High Priest* is worked in a low relief style of carving. The side walls of each area or element are rounded over with little or no shaping steps done to the main body of the elements. Remember that elements within a design are any identifiable area of the pattern. For example, this design has four hair elements—four areas where the hair can be grouped into one large cluster of hair strands.

Pattern background

The background for the patterns in this book is shown in gray. This background does not represent the size of the carving blank, but rather the carved background area of the piece.

Tools and Supplies

- 11½" x 13" x ¾" (292 x 330 x 19mm) bark-edged basswood plaque
- Bench knife
- Chip carving knife
- Large, medium, and small round gouges
- Wide sweep round gouge
- Straight chisel
- Bull-nose chisel
- Tight U-gouge
- V-gouge
- Sharpening tools and strop
- Graphite tracing paper
- Painter's tape
- Pencil or ink pen
- Dusting brush
- Clean, soft cloth
- Sandpaper, 220- and 320-grit
- Thick terrycloth towel or nonslip mat

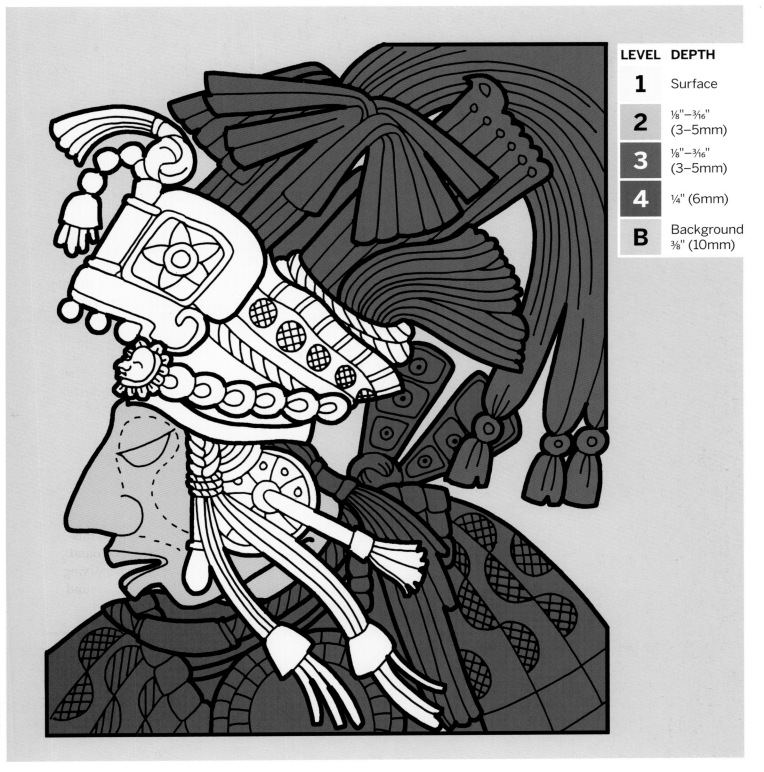

LEVEL	DEPTH
1	Surface
2	⅛"–³⁄₁₆" (3–5mm)
3	⅛"–³⁄₁₆" (3–5mm)
4	¼" (6mm)
B	Background ⅜" (10mm)

Enlarge pattern 120%.

Note: This pattern contains rough estimates of the depth measurements for each level based on the thickness of the board I used to carve this project. Remember that relief carvings should generally be worked in the top half of your wood blank. Adjust these measurements as necessary according to the thickness of the blank you're using.

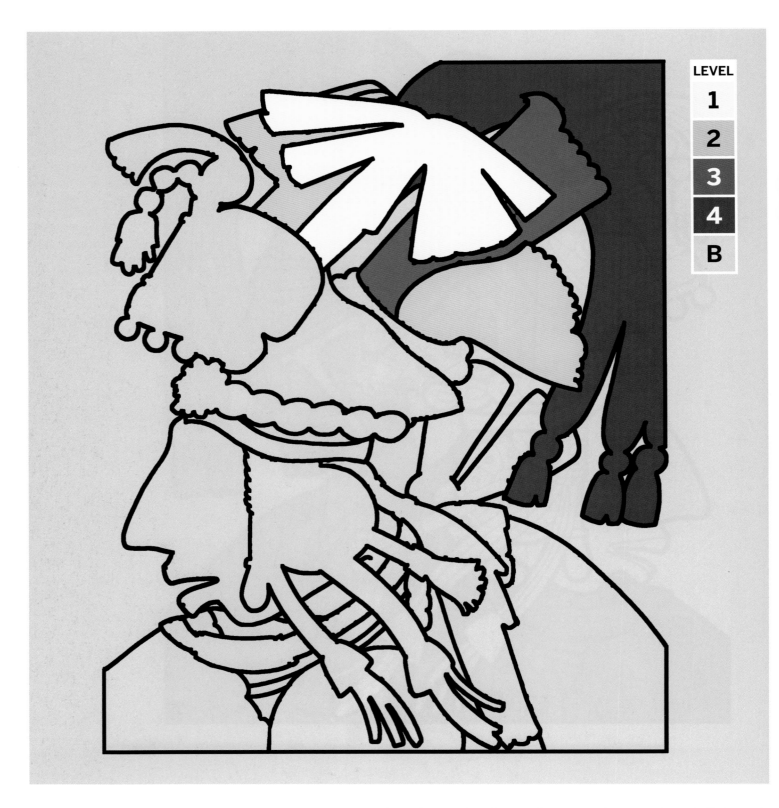

LEVEL
1
2
3
4
B

Note: These colored diagrams show the sub-levels of the hair and headdress. Use them for reference when carving these areas to create the tapered, angled effect that will give the final carving the appearance of depth.

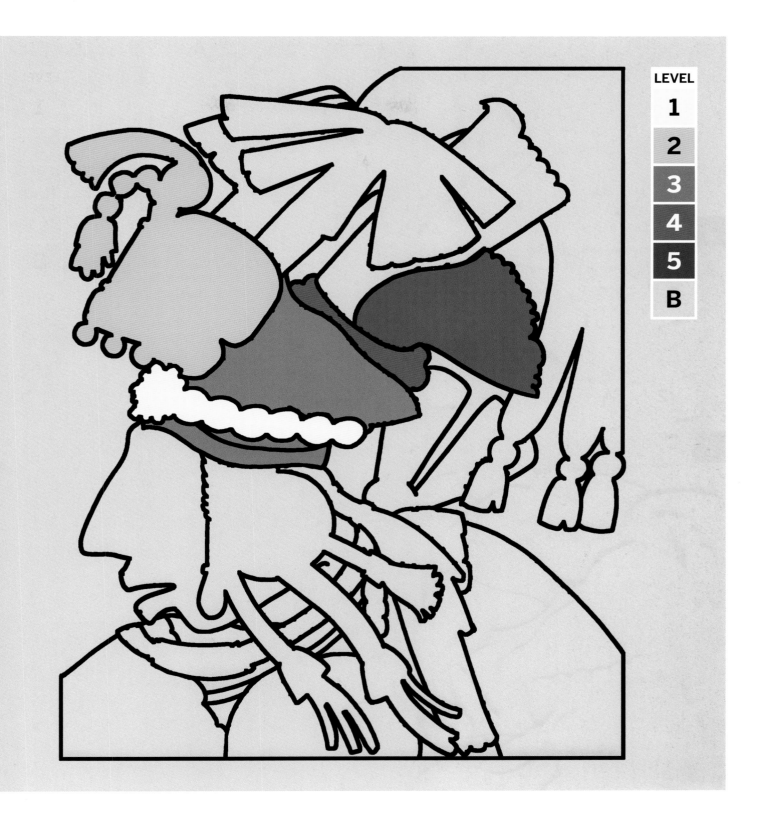

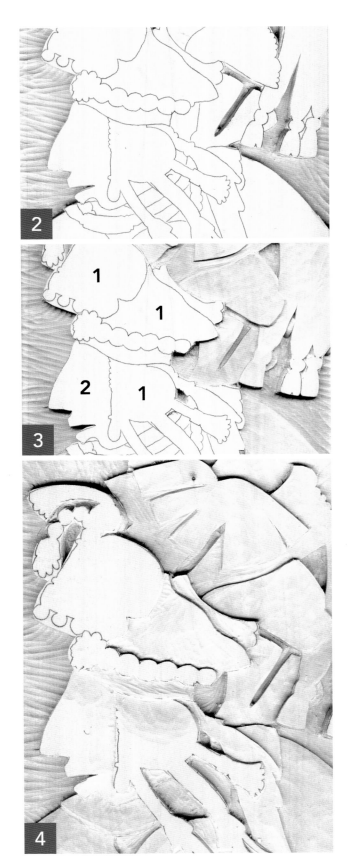

1 Prepare the blank and transfer the pattern.
Prepare your wood blank by sanding it smooth using 220-grit sandpaper. Remove any dust with a dry, clean cloth. Make a copy of the pattern. Center and tape the pattern to the board. Using graphite paper, trace the pattern lines and number each level. I have also included two sub-layer patterns that show the levels of the individual elements of the hair and headdress (see pages 72 and 73). Use these for reference when carving these areas.

2 Rough out the background. Using your bench knife, make stop cuts along the outer pattern lines to separate the design area from the background area. Using your large round gouge, cut away the wood in the background area, dropping the deepest point of the background where it touches the pattern area to ⅜" (10mm) deep. Work the round gouge strokes from the outer borders of the carving blank into the design area to create a gouge stroke halo. Tight or confined areas in the background can be rough cut using a small round gouge or tight U-gouge.

3 Mark and cut the layers to depth. Using a pencil, mark the large layers of the design on the wood blank by numbering them according to the pattern. Mark the deepest layer with a number four and the highest layer with a number one. Then, working from the lowest layer to the highest, drop each layer to its predetermined depth in the blank. The highest layer (1) can be left at this stage at the original level of the wood.

4 Shape the layers as desired and cut the elements to depth. Layers in a relief carving do not need to be flat or level. For this project, I cut many of the layers so they slant or angle toward the center point of the main design. To do this, divide each layer into smaller groups of elements. Drop each of these elements to the proper depth within their layer by creating a stop cut with a bench knife. Then, use the round gouges and straight chisel to drop each element to its depth measurement. Use chip carved triangles at the sharp corners during the stop cut stage.

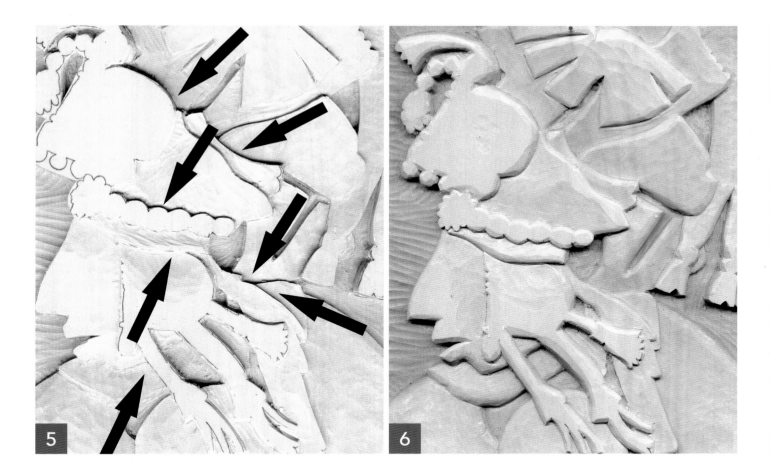

5   **Taper the design elements.** As a general
rule, relief carvings should be worked in the
top half of the wood blank, leaving the lower
half intact to provide stability. Applying this
rule to a ¾" (19mm)-thick board means the
carving should only reach ⅜" (10mm) deep at
its deepest point. This does not provide a lot of
wood to work with to give each individual level or
element its own separate depth. In this carving,
an appearance of depth is created by tapering
the smaller elements within each level so that
the area of an element that joins or intersects a
higher element is carved lower in depth than the
level as a whole. This tapering or slanting lets
you create an impression of greater depth and
more levels than the carving actually has.

6   **Shape and smooth the elements.** After each
layer has been dropped to its appropriate
depth in the wood, you are ready to shape each
element. For this project, round over the outer
edge of each element and work the center
area into a smooth gradual transition from the
highest points to the lowest points. Begin the
shaping steps by recutting each element using
as wide a round gouge as possible. Focus on
reducing the ridges left from the rough out work.
Using a straight chisel or bull-nose chisel, work
the surface of each element to remove any
remaining round gouge ridges. Round over the
edges of each element using a bench knife, chip
carving knife, or straight chisel. If needed, recut
sharp corners in the design using a V-gouge or
bench knife.

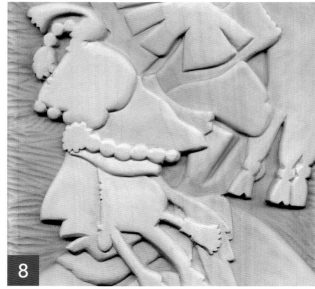

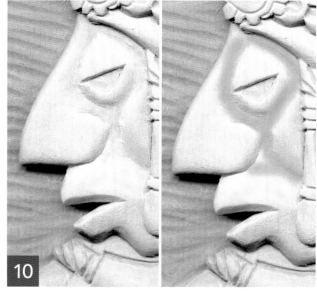

7 **Sand the elements.** After you have shaped each element with your carving tools, smooth each element and remove any wood fibers using sandpaper. Start with 220-grit sandpaper and work your way up to 320-grit sandpaper, working with the wood grain whenever possible.

8 **Check the carving for a uniform appearance.** Uncarved areas of a wood blank have a different appearance in texture and shine than carved areas. Sanded areas will also have a different look than unsanded areas. Because of this, you should treat every area of a relief carving using the same steps or processes to create a uniform sheen. During this step, check that every element surface, especially those left at the original level of the wood blank, has been carved. The high areas only need a light shaving using a wide sweep gouge or straight chisel, but they do need to be carved. You can see the carving pictured has a uniform texture and sheen. All the high areas were dressed out through shaving with a straight chisel. The entire carved area, including the round gouge background, was lightly sanded using 220-grit paper, followed by a second light sanding using 320-grit paper.

9 **Begin carving the details.** Once the sanding and smoothing steps are completed, trace or pencil in the fine line details of the design. Using a V-gouge, begin cutting along these detail lines. You can use your straight chisel to bevel some of the detail lines throughout the hair, headdress, and robe.

10 **Carve the face details.** Shape the Mayan High Priest's face using your medium and large round gouges. Note the dotted line on the pattern for this project (see page 71). This is the guideline for your round gouge work. Cut a shallow medium round gouge trough along the dotted line—around the outside of the eye and eyelids, between the nose and cheek area, and along the top of the upper lip. Using your large gouge, taper the side of the nose into the medium round gouge trough. Continue tapering the face at the cheek line into the gouge trough and at the top of the lip up toward the eye area. You can use your small round gouge to taper the slant of the face where it meets both eyelids and along the bottom edge of the cheek. Use your V-gouge to cut a shallow line at the edge of the nostrils. Cut the eye area using a stop cut, and then lower the eyeball using a small round gouge. Lightly sand the face using 320-grit sandpaper. By lowering the areas around the facial features with your round gouges, you give the face the impression of having raised eyes, cheeks, and nostrils.

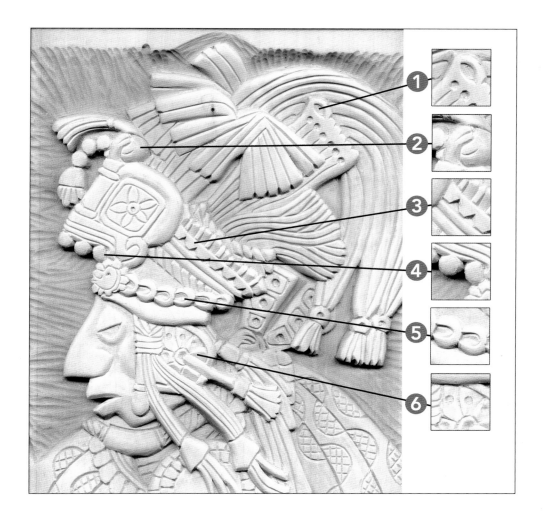

The final shaping

Because stone—the original carving medium for this image—is so very hard to work, Mayan, Incan, and Aztec stone carvers relied heavily on cut detail lines to give dimension to their hieroglyphs. As a wood carver, your carving medium is quite easy to work, so you can add some shaping to the small individual details of your design after you have worked in your detail lines.

The image above shows you a few of the shaped areas in my carving. You can work any area within your carving to add your own unique details.

1. The bird hair comb, the sun's eye, the bead details in the neck scarf, and the three long strand hair knots were carved using circle cuts created with an upended small round gouge.

2. There are two knots in this design—one at the top of the headdress and one at the back of the neck in the scarf. I shaped these yin-yang knot areas by tucking the inside sections of each side of the knot toward the center of the knot.

3. The top band of the headdress was a perfect place to shape by chisel cutting every other rectangular section lower than the adjacent rectangles to create an alternating pattern. This rolls the band in an up-then-down pattern. Below this band I chip cut triangles to form a V pattern using a bench knife and a straight chisel.

4. I shaped the large beads on the headdress into convex (half-circle) curves using my bench knife and straight chisel.

5. Using my large round gouge, I made concave dents in the lower headdress line. I used my V-gouge to cut small V-trough outlines around the outside of each gouge dent.

6. The headdress earpiece was cut into sections, much like pie slices. This was a perfect place for shaping, so I used my straight chisel to taper each section (pie slice) into the next.

Painting and antiquing your project

I chose to use acrylic and oil paints to bring some bright color to my carving. Using acrylic colors for basswood carvings is easy and quick. Because this type of paint is opaque, mistakes can be corrected by allowing the painted area to dry completely and then applying the new, correct color over top.

Painting and Antiquing Supplies

- Acrylic craft paints in:
  - Off-White
  - Raw Sienna
  - Burnt Sienna
  - Yellow Ochre
  - Cadmium Orange Medium
  - Cadmium Red Medium
  - Cadmium Yellow
  - Deep Jade Green
  - Medium Turquoise
  - Burnt Umber
  - Ultramarine Blue
  - Carbon Black
- Oil paints in:
  - Burnt Umber
  - Carbon Black
  - Off-White or Antique White
- Soft-bristle paintbrushes, including shader, round, and detail brushes
- Toothbrush or splatter brush
- Water
- Glass tile, palette paper, or tinfoil
- Large antiquing brush
- Clean, lint-free wiping cloths
- Turpentine
- Polyurethane spray sealer
- Green or blue painter's tape or transparent tape
- Fine-point permanent marker

1 Paint on a primer coat. Basswood, with its very plain white grain, is an excellent wood for colored carvings, but because basswood is very soft, it is also very absorbent. Basswood therefore requires a primer coat to be applied before the actual colors can be added. Primer coats are worked using a craft water-based acrylic paint and used to cover the entire area of a carving that will be painted. Often a primer coat is painted using white or off-white colors, but medium brown, pale brown, and pale gray are excellent primer colors, especially for projects you want to paint with true hues or jewel-toned colors. Because this piece represents a stone carving, I applied a primer coat in medium golden brown. To create this primer, begin by mixing one part off-white acrylic paint with one part raw sienna. Thin this paint mixture with a quarter part water, and then apply two even coats to the carved area. Allow the primer coat to dry thoroughly.

2 Mix the paint colors with the primer and apply.
Sometimes, when painting, it can be difficult to
choose a color palette that is both complementary
to the carving as well as coordinated for a uniform
effect. To coordinate or unite all the paint colors for
this stone carving reproduction, mix one part of each
color (directly from the paint tube) with one part of
the primer coat mixture. This will give every color a
soft beige tone and the same pale tonal value. To mix
the colors, place a brush full of primer color on your
tinfoil or palette paper. Add one brush of color directly
from the paint tube to the primer color and mix well.
Brush one to two coats of the new color on the area of
the carving to be painted.

3 Check your progress. As you color each element,
take a moment to turn your carving upside down
to check that all of the walls of the area have been
coated. If you make a mistake, go outside the area
you intended to paint, or simply want to change
the color of an area you have already painted, let
the first color dry completely, and then repaint the
area. Because the painting steps for this project
also include speckling and antiquing, you do not
need to have pristine, crisp color edges between
each element.

4 Speckle the carving with paint. Stones have
many colors, color tones, cracks, and even spotting
patterns. Few stones are one uniform color
throughout. To give this carving color changes and
patterns similar to those that might be found in stone,
you can apply several speckled coats of splatter work
to the piece. To protect the bark edge of the plaque
as you do this, place several pieces of painter's tape
or transparent tape over the bark edge areas of
the carving. Then, on a tile or piece of tinfoil, place
a small amount of burnt umber, deep jade green,
yellow ochre, off-white, and carbon black acrylic
paint. Dampen an old toothbrush with clean water.
Pick up a small amount of color from the tile on the
tip of the toothbrush. Hold the brush over the carving
and use your thumb to pull backward on the brush
bristles. This will cause a fine spray of small paint
droplets to be transferred to the carving. To create
fine, extremely small droplets, use as little water on
your brush as possible—more water creates large
splatters, while less water creates small splatters.
Work a layer of splatter for each color on your palette.
Allow the splattering to dry, and then remove the
protective tape from the bark edges.

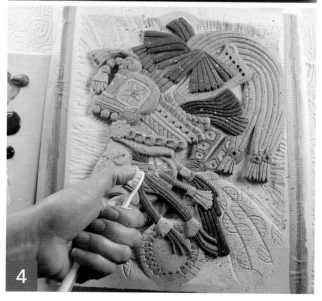

5

6

5 **Apply a sealer.** After the acrylic paint has dried completely, the carving is ready for an application of two to three light, even coats of polyurethane spray sealer. You can use sealer with a gloss, semi-gloss, or matte finish; I prefer a gloss coating as my protective layer before antiquing. Follow the manufacturer's instructions for applying the sealer. Turn your carving with each new coat to ensure that you have covered the deep areas, walls, and V-cut troughs of the carving. Let the polyurethane sealer dry for several hours before you move on to the antiquing steps. When applied to damp sealer, the turpentine in the oil paints you will use to antique the carving can cause the sealer to become cloudy. On the back of your wood plaque, sign and date the project using a fine-point permanent marker.

6 **Antique the carving.** Place a small amount (about the size of a nickel coin) of burnt umber, carbon black, and off-white or antique white oil paint on your tinfoil palette. Mix the colors together well to produce a medium brown/gray color. Thin this mixture slightly with turpentine for easy brush application. Using a large antiquing brush, apply one coat of this antiquing mixture to the carved areas of the project—do not antique the bark edge. With a soft, clean, lint-free cloth, wipe the surface of the carving to remove the antiquing color from the high areas of the work. You can spot antique when you use oil paints by applying the antiquing mix to small 3" x 3" (76 x 76mm) areas at a time, and then wiping the areas clean. This gives you more control over the final stain color and how much stain builds up in one area. Because oil paints dry more slowly than acrylics, the small areas you worked can easily be blended with one another. If you want one area of the carving to be antiqued, but do not want the antiquing effect in another area, fold your wiping cloth to a clean section. Then, wipe the carving, working from the area you do not want to be antiqued into the area where you want the antiquing effect. To ensure the carving has an even antique finish, fold your wiping cloth to a dirty area, and then wipe the entire surface of the carving using that portion of the cloth. The small amount of antiquing mixture left on the cloth will blend all the oil paints on the surface of the carving evenly. Allow the antique mixture to dry thoroughly, preferably for several days, and then reseal the work using polyurethane spray sealer.

PROJECT:
Mexican Toucans

Simple Rounded-Over Edge Carving
Low Relief

This family of toucans is worked in four simple steps: rough out the background, create the layers, round over the edges, and add the details. The steps are worked following the same exact same process as that employed for the *Mayan High Priest* project (page 70).

Supplies:

- 9" x 13" x ¾" (229 x 330 x 19mm) bark-edged basswood plaque
- Bench knife
- Large and small round gouges
- Wide sweep round gouge

- V-gouge
- Straight chisel
- Sharpening tools and strop
- Stiff toothbrush or stiff dusting brush
- Clean, soft cloth

- 220-grit sandpaper
- Graphite tracing paper
- Painter's tape
- Pencil
- Thick terrycloth towel or nonslip mat

LEVEL	DEPTH
1	Surface
2	1/16" (2mm)
3	1/8 (3mm)
4	3/16" (5mm)
B	Background 3/8" (10mm)

Enlarge pattern 115%.

Note: This pattern contains rough estimates of the depth measurements for each level based on the thickness of the board I used to carve this project. Remember that relief carvings should generally be worked in the top half of your wood blank. Adjust these measurements as necessary according to the thickness of the blank you're using.

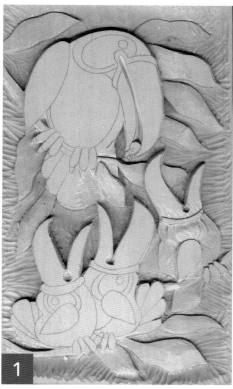

1 **Transfer the pattern and rough out the background.** Transfer the pattern to the basswood plaque using graphite paper. Stop cut along the edges of the pattern lines in the background area of the wood using a V-gouge or bench knife. Use round gouges to cut into the stop cuts. Work the background to a depth of ⅜" (10mm).

2 **Mark and cut the layers to depth.** Following the pattern, mark each layer with its corresponding number, four being the deepest layer of the carving, and one being the highest. Rough out each layer to its depth, using the depth gauge as a guide.

3 **Round over the edges of the elements.** Using a bench knife, straight chisel, or wide sweep round gouge, round over the edges of each of the design's elements, giving a gentle roll to each one. Smooth each area by shaving it with a straight chisel. Lightly sand the carving using 220-grit sandpaper.

4 **Add in the details.** Retrace or pencil in the fine detail lines of the design. With a bench knife or V-gouge, cut the detail lines. Using a straight chisel, bevel or shape some areas along the detail lines as desired.

5 **Clean up the carving.** Rub the surface of the carving with a stiff toothbrush or stiff dusting brush to remove any loose wood fibers. Lightly sand, if necessary, using 220-grit sandpaper, and remove the sanding dust with a soft, clean cloth.

Painting your project

I thought these tropical birds needed some bright coloring, so I finished my carving with acrylic craft paints. To begin painting your project, apply one to two light coats of white primer to the layers of the carving, leaving the background area and bark edge of the plaque unpainted. Allow the primer to dry well.

Place your craft paints on a clean glazed tile. Using soft-bristle brushes and the project photo as a guide, apply one to two coats of the following colors to the following areas of the design:

- Titanium white: inner belly ring
- Cadmium yellow medium: top of the beak, outer eye ring, second belly ring
- Cadmium orange: third from top beak line for the adult, mouth edge of the beak for the chicks
- Cadmium red medium: mouth edge of the adult beak, outer belly ring, inside area of the tail feathers
- Medium verde green: dark leaves (see photo for placement)
- Light verde green: inner eye rings, second beak stripe on top beak, bottom beak stripe on bottom beak
- Mix equal parts light verde green and cadmium yellow medium: light leaves (the remaining unpainted leaves)
- Carbon black: head ring, body areas, wings, outer rings of tail feathers
- Medium teal blue: front half of the bottom beak stripe, toes
- Lightly touch some medium teal blue to the tops of the wings and the tops of the body areas
- Mix equal parts medium teal blue with titanium white and apply to the top of each toe

Allow the paint to dry well. Then, apply two light coats of polyurethane spray sealer to the entire project and allow it to dry. Following the manufacturer's instructions, apply one coat of mahogany oil stain to the carved areas of the plaque. Wipe the carving well with a clean, soft cloth to remove the excess stain. Allow the stain to dry well.

Seal the work with one to two light coats of polyurethane spray sealer.

Painting Supplies

- Acrylic or craft paints in:
  - Titanium White
  - Cadmium Yellow Medium
  - Cadmium Orange
  - Cadmium Red Medium
  - Medium Verde Green
  - Light Verde Green
  - Carbon Black
  - Medium Teal Blue
- Polyurethane spray sealer
- Glass tile, palette paper, or tinfoil
- Clean, soft cloth
- Mahogany oil stain
- Water
- Assorted soft-bristle paintbrushes
- Soft, clean antiquing brush
- Turpentine or mineral spirits

PROJECT:
Celtic Stone Dragon

Simple Rounded Shaping
Low Relief

Not all relief carvings have multiple levels or layers. In this carving there are only two levels: the background surrounding the dragon and the dragon itself. After the background has been rough cut, the dragon's body can be shaped in specific areas to create the over-and-under effect of a Celtic knot pattern.

Supplies:

- 8" x 10" x ¾" (203 x 254 x 19mm) router-edged basswood plaque
- Bench knife
- Large and small round gouges
- Wide sweep round gouge
- V-gouge
- Straight chisel
- Sharpening tools and strop
- 220-grit sandpaper
- Graphite tracing paper
- Painter's tape
- Pencil
- Ruler and/or compass
- Soft, clean cloth
- Stiff toothbrush or brass wire brush
- Thick terrycloth towel or nonslip mat

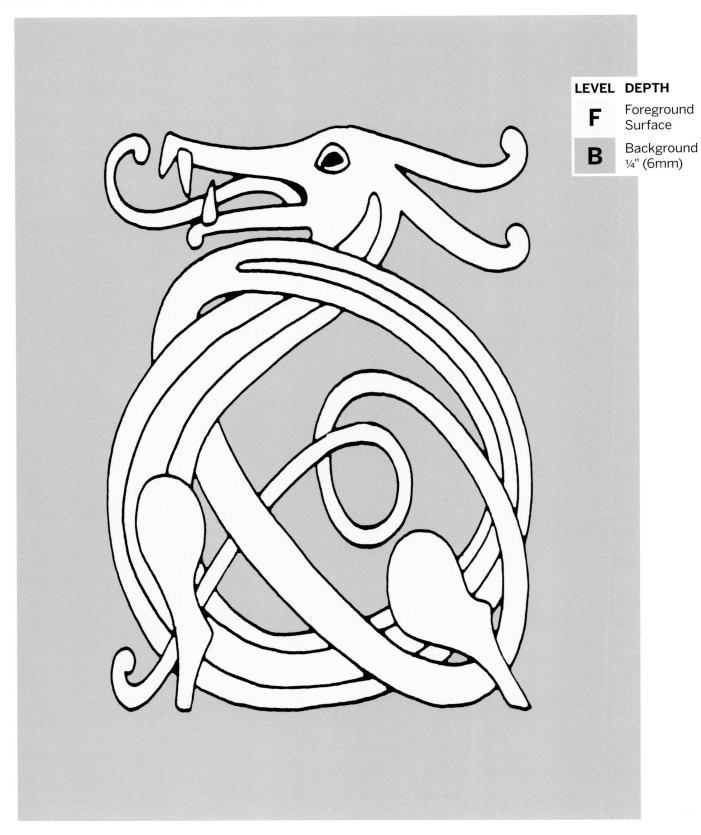

LEVEL	DEPTH
F	Foreground Surface
B	Background ¼" (6mm)

Pattern shown at 100%.

Note: This pattern contains rough estimates of the depth measurements for each level based on the thickness of the board I used to carve this project. Remember that relief carvings should generally be worked in the top half of your wood blank. Adjust these measurements as necessary according to the thickness of the blank you're using.

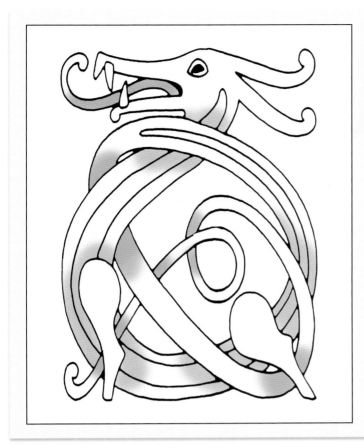

Celtic and Viking knot patterns were originally carved in stone with a minimal amount of shaping. For this carving, shaping is worked on the areas of the dragon's body that are tucked under other sections of the body. Follow the gray shading shown here as you work the shaping steps for this carving.

1 **Transfer the pattern and rough out the background.** Make a copy of the dragon pattern, and center and tape it to the plaque. Using graphite paper, trace the design (including the detail lines) onto the wood. Use a ruler or compass to mark a margin line ¼" (6mm) from the routed edge of the board on all four sides. Make stop cuts along the outside lines of the pattern and the margin lines. Rough cut the background area to a depth of ¼" (6mm) using a round gouge or wide sweep gouge. Smooth some, but not all, of the high ridges left from the round gouge cuts—the background of the finished piece should have some gouge texturing.

2 **Begin shaping the dragon.** Using a V-gouge, make stop cuts along the inner pattern lines of the body of the dragon. Use a large round gouge and/or straight chisel to taper the areas of the dragon's body that are tucked under other sections of the dragon's body.

3 **Smooth the transitions and cut the eye.** To create a smooth transition from a high area of the dragon's body as it rolls under another section, shave the body using a straight chisel. This extends the taper from the high area to the low area into a shallow, sloping ramp. Use a straight chisel to bevel the edges of each area. Cut the dragon's eye by upending a small round gouge and cutting the outline of a circle. Remove the circle chip with a bench knife.

4 **Finish shaping the dragon.** Continue shaping the body and edges of the dragon using a straight chisel. Recut the intersection lines between the body sections with a V-gouge where necessary.

5 **Clean up the carving and add texture.** Lightly sand the carving using 220-grit sandpaper. Leave some of the ridges from carving in both the dragon and background areas to give the carving a stone-like textured look. Remove the sanding dust using a dry, clean cloth. Add extra texture to the dragon's body and background areas by brushing the carving with a stiff toothbrush or brass wire brush.

6 **Mark and carve the scale design.** With a soft #2 pencil, mark the checkered line pattern on the body and legs of the dragon. Use a V-gouge to make shallow V-cuts along the pencil lines to carve these textured areas. Dust the carving well afterward with a stiff toothbrush or brass wire brush.

Painting and Finishing Supplies

- Acrylic craft paints in:
  - Titanium White
  - Carbon Black
  - Payne's Gray
  - Burnt Umber
  - Burnt Sienna
- Driftwood oil stain
- Water
- Glass tile, palette paper, or tinfoil
- Paper towels
- Clean, soft cloth
- Assorted soft-bristle paintbrushes
- Splatter brush or old toothbrush
- Masking tape or painter's tape
- 220-grit sandpaper
- Polyurethane spray sealer

Painting and finishing your project

Use several strips of painter's tape or masking tape to protect the routed edges of the carving. Place a small amount of titanium white, Payne's gray, and burnt umber on a glass tile. Thin each color with an equal amount of clean water.

Brush two wash coats of titanium white on the carved area of the plaque. Because you mixed equal parts paint and water, these coats will not give full, solid coverage.

While the titanium white coats are still damp, pick up a small amount of Payne's gray and mix it with the titanium white on your tile. Working along the diagonal of the plaque, brush a few random strokes of the gray/white mix over the white background. Pick up a little more Payne's gray, add it to the gray/white mix and repeat the application to the carving. Next, add a small touch of burnt umber to the gray/white mix and repeat. Add a small amount of burnt sienna to the mix and repeat. Your background should now contain many shades of white, gray, and brown. Allow these coatings to dry for about half an hour.

Clean your glass tile, and then place a small amount of each paint color on the tile. Do not thin these colors with water. Working one color at a time, use an old stiff toothbrush or splatter brush to splatter a coat of each color on the carving. Do this by picking up a small amount of color on the end of the splatter brush. Hold the brush a few inches from the surface of the carving and pull your thumb across the top of the brush. This action will spray a fine mist of paint drops over the carving. Thin the paint with a few drops of water if you wish to create a large splatter or dot pattern.

Remove the tape from the edges of the carving. Brush two thinned wash coats of titanium white on the routed border edges of the plaque. Streak this area with a mix of titanium white and Payne's gray, just as you did with the center of the carving. Allow the carving to dry overnight.

After you have completed the painting steps and allowed the paint to dry, sand the carved areas, background, and routed edges of the plaque using 220-grit sandpaper to remove some paint from the high areas of the carving. Sand lightly in some areas to remove one or two layers of color; in other areas, sand the carving back to the raw wood. Clean the dust from the board using a soft, dry cloth.

Seal the work with two coats of polyurethane spray sealer. Allow the sealer to dry thoroughly. Follow the manufacturer's instructions to apply an oil-based stain to the carving. Wipe away the excess oil stain with a soft, clean cloth. Allow the stain to dry overnight. Seal the work with one to two light coats of polyurethane spray sealer. Sign and date the back of the plaque when finished.

PROJECT:
Beta Fish

Concave and Convex Curves
Realistic Relief

Using a combination of concave and convex curves,
a realistic style of shaping can be worked in your
relief carving projects.

Tools and Supplies:

- 8" x 10" x ¾" (203 x 254 x 19mm) bark-edged basswood plaque
- V-gouge
- Large and small round gouges
- Wide sweep round gouge
- Straight chisel

- Bench knife or chip carving knife
- Sharpening tools and strop
- Graphite tracing paper
- Painter's tape
- Pencil

- 220-grit sandpaper
- Stiff toothbrush or brass wire brush
- Clean, soft cloth
- Thick terrycloth towel or nonslip mat

LEVEL	DEPTH
1	Surface
2	¹⁄₁₆" (2mm)
3	⅛" (3mm)
4	³⁄₁₆" (5mm)
B	Background ⅜" (10mm)

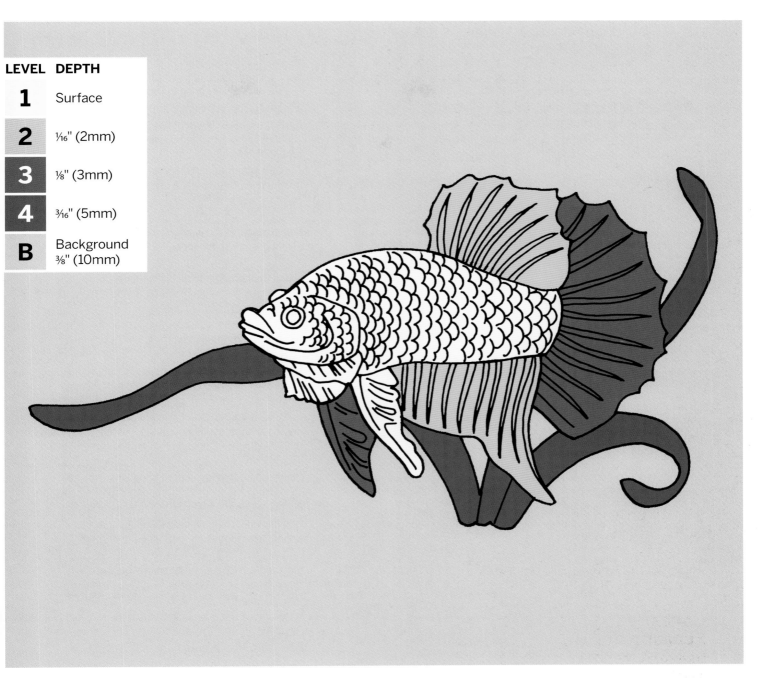

Pattern shown at 100%.

Note: This pattern contains rough estimates of the depth measurements for each level based on the thickness of the board I used to carve this project. Remember that relief carvings should generally be worked in the top half of your wood blank. Adjust these measurements as necessary according to the thickness of the blank you're using.

1 Prepare the carving blank and transfer the pattern. Prepare the basswood plaque by lightly sanding the working surface with 220-grit sandpaper. Make a copy of the simplified pattern and transfer it to the carving blank using graphite paper.

2 Rough out the background. The background to this carving is tapered from the outer edges in toward the beta fish and leaves. To create this taper, make stop cuts along the outer lines of the beta pattern. Then, use a large round gouge or wide sweep gouge to rough cut the background area. Make the first background cuts about 1"–1½" (25–38mm) from the fish. As you lower the area with more round gouge cuts, start each new grouping of cuts about ½" (13mm) further away from the previous grouping. This process will create a natural, slow, smooth taper.

3 Cut and shape the elements. Cut along the pattern lines of each element (fins, tail, and gills) with a V-gouge. Use a straight chisel and a large round gouge to roll each area into its general curved shape. Give the leaves and body area of the fish a convex shape and the fins a concave shape. Use the straight chisel or wide sweep gouge to shave each area until it is as smooth as possible. Upend your small round gouge to cut the outline of a circle for the eye. Shape the eye and lower the face area near the eye with a large round gouge and straight chisel.

4 Add in the details. With a pencil, mark the lines for the fin and tail ribs. Use a small round gouge to make long, half-circle cuts between these lines. Make these cuts the entire length of each fin/tail area, with the deepest point of the gouge cut at the base of the fin where it connects to the fish body. Mark the rib lines in the lower gill and the front fins. Use the V-gouge to cut a shallow trough along each of these pencil lines. Add a few thin, shallow V-gouge cuts to the tail and the large upper and lower fins. Upend your small round gouge to make a shallow profile cut for each fish scale (if desired, draw in a few light pencil guidelines before you begin this step). Cut each scale by pushing the round gouge straight into the wood for a shallow cut and then lifting the gouge straight up off the wood. Cut the mouth lines using a V-gouge. Lightly sand the carving with 220-grit sandpaper to remove any loose wood fibers. Remove the sanding dust with a clean, dry cloth.

Painting your project

1 **Seal the carving and apply a base coat.** To seal the wood to keep it from absorbing excess acrylic paint, apply two light coats of polyurethane spray sealer. Allow the sealer to dry for at least half an hour. On a glass tile or palette paper, combine equal parts burnt umber paint and water. Brush one to two light coats of this mixture on the fish and leaves. Do not apply paint to the background area. Allow the paint to dry.

2 **Finish the carving.** Thin a small amount of the remaining paint colors with an equal amount of water. Apply one light coat of cadmium red medium to the body and the base of the tail and fins. While this coat is still damp, shade these areas with cadmium yellow medium and titanium white. Apply a light coat of medium verde green to the leaves, and add titanium white shading to the leaf tips. Paint the eye with one to two light coats of carbon black. Allow the carving to dry thoroughly—preferably overnight. Sign and date the back of the carving with a fine-point permanent marker. Seal the wood using two coats of polyurethane spray sealer.

Painting Supplies
- Acrylic craft paints in:
  - Burnt Umber
  - Cadmium Red Medium
  - Cadmium Yellow Medium
  - Medium Verde Green
  - Carbon Black
  - Titanium White
- Assorted soft-bristle paintbrushes
- Water
- Polyurethane spray sealer
- Glass tile, palette paper, or tinfoil
- Fine-point permanent marker

PROJECT:
Sunken Greenman

Sunken Low Relief

For this project the background wood—the wood outside the pattern—is left at the original level of the wood surface. Only the actual design area is carved, creating the appearance that it is sunk into the wood in the final carving.

Tools and Supplies:

- 9" x 12" x ¾" basswood plaque (229 x 305 x 19mm)
- Bench knife
- Chip carving knife
- Large and small round gouges
- Straight chisel
- Wide sweep round gouge
- V-gouge

- Bull-nose chisel
- Sharpening tools and strop
- 220-grit sandpaper
- Soft, clean cloth
- Sanding sealer
- Graphite tracing paper
- Painter's tape

- Pencil
- Ruler
- Polyurethane spray sealer
- Pecan oil stain
- Fine-point permanent marker
- Thick terrycloth towel or nonslip mat

LEVEL	DEPTH
1	Surface
2	¼" (6mm)
3	⅜" (10mm)
4	½" (13mm)

Enlarge pattern 125%.

Note: This pattern contains rough estimates of the depth measurements for each level based on the thickness of the board I used to carve this project. Remember that relief carvings should generally be worked in the top half of your wood blank. Adjust these measurements as necessary according to the thickness of the blank you're using.

1 **Transfer the pattern and cut the outlines.**
Prepare your board by lightly sanding it with 220-grit sandpaper. Remove the sanding dust with a dry, clean cloth. Make a copy of the pattern, center it, and tape it to the board. Trace the pattern using graphite paper. Using a pencil and ruler, measure and mark a border line ½" (13mm) from the edges on all four sides of the blank. Measure and mark a second border line ¾" (19mm) from the edges on all four sides. With the V-gouge, make stop cuts along the outer pattern lines of the face and along both border lines. With a straight chisel, bevel the sides of the border line cuts.

2 **Cut and shape the background leaves.** Use a bench knife to create stop cuts along the pattern lines of the face side of the lowest leaf clusters (around the mouth and mustache). With a large and/or small round gouge, rough cut the background leaves, tapering them from their highest point at the outer edge of the pattern to their lowest point where they intersect with the face and upper leaf clusters.

3 **Smooth the background leaves and cut and shape the mouth leaves.** Use a wide sweep gouge or large round gouge to remove the ridges left from the rough out work on the background leaves. With the bench knife, work stop cuts along the leaves extending from the mouth. Cut these leaves to depth with a straight chisel and round over the edges. With a V-gouge, create a center vein in each leaf by making a V-cut. Round over the lips with a straight chisel.

4 **Cut the outline for the eyelids.** Using a V-gouge, stop cut around the upper and lower eyelids.

5 **Shape the eyeballs.** Use a straight chisel or wide sweep round gouge to round over the eyeballs.

6 **Shape the eyebrows.** Shape the upper eyebrow area of the face with a straight chisel or a wide sweep gouge.

7 **Shape the face.** Create a stop cut with the V-gouge from the corner of each eye to the side of the face. Round over the edges of the face with a straight chisel. Round over and shape the area above and below the eyelids with a straight chisel.

8 **Carve the pupils.** Upend a large round gouge at the top of each eye to cut the outline of a three-quarter circle. Remove the circle chips with a bench knife. This creates indented circles to represent the pupils of the eyes.

9 **Shape the cheeks.** Stop cut along the sides of the nose with a V-gouge. Shape the sides of the face next to the nose (the cheeks) with a straight chisel or a wide sweep gouge.

10 **Carve the nostrils.** Upend a small round gouge and cut the outline of a three-quarter circle for each nostril. Remove the wood from the outline cut with a bench knife.

11 Shape the nose. Shape the nose using a straight chisel, tapering it to its lowest point at the bridge.

12 Add in the facial details. With a V-gouge, cut wrinkle lines at the corner of the eyes, under the eyes, and from the corner of the nostrils into the lower cheek area. Also complete the final shaping of the mustache leaves, eyebrow leaves, and the leaves at the top of the nose.

13 Mark the background detail. Using a pencil, mark the detail leaf lines in the lower section of facial leaves.

14 **Cut the background detail.** Create stop cuts along the pencil lines using a V-gouge. With a straight chisel, bevel one side of each leaf to tuck it under the leaf above it.

15 **Smooth and sand the carving.** Smooth the carving by shaving the carved areas with a wide sweep gouge, bull-nose chisel, or straight chisel. Lightly sand the carving using 220-grit sandpaper, and remove the dust with a dry, clean cloth. Spray two coats of sanding sealer over the entire carving, following the manufacturer's instructions. Sand after each coat. Sign and date the back of the carving with a fine-point permanent marker.

16 **Finish the carving.** Following the manufacturer's instructions, apply one coat of pecan oil stain to the carving. Work small areas about 3" (76mm) square at a time, and then wipe the carving with a dry, clean cloth. Allow the stain to dry completely. Seal the work with two light coats of polyurethane spray sealer.

PROJECT:
African Mask 1

Cutting Textures and Adding Accents
Low Relief

Whether you are working in low or high relief, creating texture is a major part of the craft. This *African Mask 1* carving is first worked to a smooth, even finish, and then textured using a bench knife, round gouge, and V-gouge. The pattern can be carved over and over again, using different texturing and cut line designs in the face and collar areas to create a completely new mask every time.

Tools and Supplies:

- 15" x 11" x ¾" (381 x 279 x 19mm) router-edged basswood oval plaque
- Bench knife
- Chip carving knife
- Large and small round gouges
- Wide sweep round gouge

- Straight chisel
- Bull-nose chisel
- Tight U-gouge
- V-gouge
- Soft, clean cloth
- Sharpening tools and strop
- Compass

- Graphite tracing paper
- Painter's tape
- Pencil or ink pen
- Dusting brush
- Sandpaper, 220- and 320-grit
- Thick terrycloth towel or nonslip mat

LEVEL	DEPTH
1	Surface
2	⅜" (10mm)
3	⅜" (10mm)
4	⁷⁄₁₆" (11mm)
B	Background

Enlarge pattern 125%.

Note: This pattern contains rough estimates of the depth measurements for each level based on the thickness of the board I used to carve this project. Remember that relief carvings should generally be worked in the top half of your wood blank. Adjust these measurements as necessary according to the thickness of the blank you're using.

1 **Transfer the pattern and mark a border line.**
Prepare the oval plaque by giving it a light sanding using 220-grit sandpaper. Remove the sanding dust with a clean, dry cloth. Make a copy of the pattern, and center and tape it to the plaque. Using graphite paper, trace the outlines of the pattern onto the plaque. Then, open the legs of a compass ¼" (6mm). Place the point leg of the compass along the outer top edge of the plaque, with the pencil point against the face of the board. Use the compass to create a ¼" (6mm) border line around the edge of the plaque.

2 **Cut and taper the elements.** Use a bench knife to create stop cuts along the outer edge of the face oval, the grass elements along the left side, and along the edge of the outer collar piece. With a large round gouge, round out the background wood, tapering the walls of the background from the highest point at the pencil border line to the lowest point at the edge of the face oval. Using a bench knife, stop cut along the outlines of the facial features. Using a large round gouge, drop the face in the forehead, cheeks, and chin, tapering the level from ⅛" (3mm) deep along the edges of the facial features to ⅜" (10mm) deep at the inner edge of the face oval. Because the taper of the background and face falls so quickly to the walls of the face oval, make sure you use a bench knife for these stop cuts and rough out steps. A V-gouge may be too large to fit within the space to create a clean cut. Make stop cuts along the outlines of the inner collar piece at the face oval and taper this element into the face oval using a large round gouge. Repeat this step for the outer collar piece, ears, earrings, and grass elements along the left side. I only carved an earring in one ear. You can carve an earring in both ears or just one ear, as you prefer.

3 **Smooth and shape the elements.** Use a straight chisel, wide sweep round gouge, and/or bull-nose chisel to shave the face smooth. Smooth the collar pieces by shaving off thin slices with a large round gouge. Using a straight chisel, round over the eyes, lips, and sides of the nose. Using a V-gouge, cut along the two horizontal lines running across the eyes to create the impression of eyelids. Repeat this step for the two lines running across the lips. Shape the sides of the ears, using a straight chisel to gently round over the edges. Upend your large round gouge to make an outline cut for the hole in the left earlobe. Separate the earring wire from the collar pieces with V-cuts, and round over the edges of the earring wire and ball with a straight chisel. If you are carving two earrings, repeat this shaping with the other ear and earring.

4 **Add in the details.** Use a V-gouge to make V-cuts along the pattern lines of the grass elements at the left ear, and round over the edges of each element using a straight chisel. Round over the outer edge of the face oval with a straight chisel. Lightly recut the V-gouge lines around each of the facial features. Use 220-grit sandpaper to sand the face smooth. Also use the sandpaper to round over the high points of the gouge ridges in the background area. Remove the sanding dust with a dry, clean cloth.

5 **Add texture.** African mask carvings present a wonderful opportunity to experiment with the numerous textures and cut line patterns you can create in relief carving. For this carving, I made long curved lines in the forehead area using a V-gouge, as well as small chip-carved triangles using a bench knife (or chip carving knife). I upended my large round gouge to create a string of indented holes along the cheeks, and upended my tight U-gouge to create a small dot effect above the mouth. Above the eyes and below the mouth, I cut a series of shallow U-gouge troughs. I decorated the collar by upending a large round gouge to make circle profile cuts with added V-gouge lines to create a flower petal effect. I cut the top edge of the inner collar piece with small V-shaped strokes using a bench knife.

Painting and embellishing your project

On a glass tile or palette paper, mix three parts titanium white and one part burnt umber to create a medium beige color. Thin the mixture with a few drops of water. Brush two even coats of the mixture onto the carved surface of the board and allow the paint to dry. Place a small amount of carbon black paint on the tile and thin it with a few drops of water. Brush two coats of black to the routed edge of the plaque. Allow the paint to dry.

Place a small amount of cadmium red medium on the tile and thin it with an equal amount of water. Brush one to two light coats of this mixture to several areas of the face texture. Repeat this step with the yellow ochre, raw sienna, and ultramarine blue colors. Allow these coats to dry.

Spray the carving with two coats of polyurethane spray sealer. Allow it to dry thoroughly. Mix equal parts burnt umber paint and water. Working a small area of the carving at a time, brush one coat of this mixture onto the carving, and then wipe away the excess with a clean, dry cloth to create an antiqued effect of dark brown in the textured areas of the work. Allow the paint to dry well, and then apply a final coat of polyurethane spray sealer.

Turn the work over and sign and date the back with a fine-point permanent marker.

To add to the folk-art style of this carving, I chose to use a hot glue gun to create a small arrangement of natural fibers on the left side of the mask. I began the arrangement by cutting several bamboo sticks longer than the distance from the ear area to the border edge of the carving. This brought the arrangement beyond the edges of the wood plaque. I used hot glue to secure the bamboo in place. Next, I added several long strands of thick gray cotton twine, several long reed grass curls, and two groupings of raffia over the bamboo. To complete the arrangement, I added some ivory saved from a few old piano keys and two different types of seashells.

Lightly sand the carving using 220-grit sandpaper and remove any dust with a clean, dry cloth.

Painting and Embellishing Supplies

- Acrylic craft paints in:
  - Titanium White
  - Cadmium Red Medium
  - Yellow Ochre
  - Raw Sienna
  - Ultramarine Blue
  - Burnt Umber
  - Carbon Black
- Polyurethane spray sealer
- Soft, clean cloth
- 220-grit sandpaper
- Assorted soft-bristle paintbrushes
- Water
- Glass tile, palette paper, or tinfoil
- Hot glue and hot glue gun
- Assorted natural fibers, such as bamboo sticks, raffia, cotton twine, bird's nest moss, reed grass, feathers, or small seashells
- Fine-point permanent marker

PROJECT:
African Mask 2

Deep Low Relief

The technique of low relief carving, with its rounded walls and exposed element joint lines, can be worked on wood of any thickness. This carving is worked identically to *African Mask 1*, but the blank for this carving is 2" (51mm) thick, allowing for greater depth than in *African Mask 1*.

Tools and Supplies

- 16" x 12" x 2" (406 x 305 x 51mm) bark-edged basswood plaque
- V-gouge
- Large and small round gouges
- Straight chisel
- Bull-nose chisel
- Small round chisel
- Tight U-gouge

- Bench knife or chip carving knife
- Sharpening tools and strop
- Ruler or compass
- 2"–3" (51–76mm) jar lids
- Soft, clean cloth
- Graphite tracing paper
- Painter's tape

- Pencil
- 220-grit sandpaper
- Stiff toothbrush or brass wire brush
- Sanding sealer
- Polyurethane spray sealer
- Thick terrycloth towel or nonslip mat

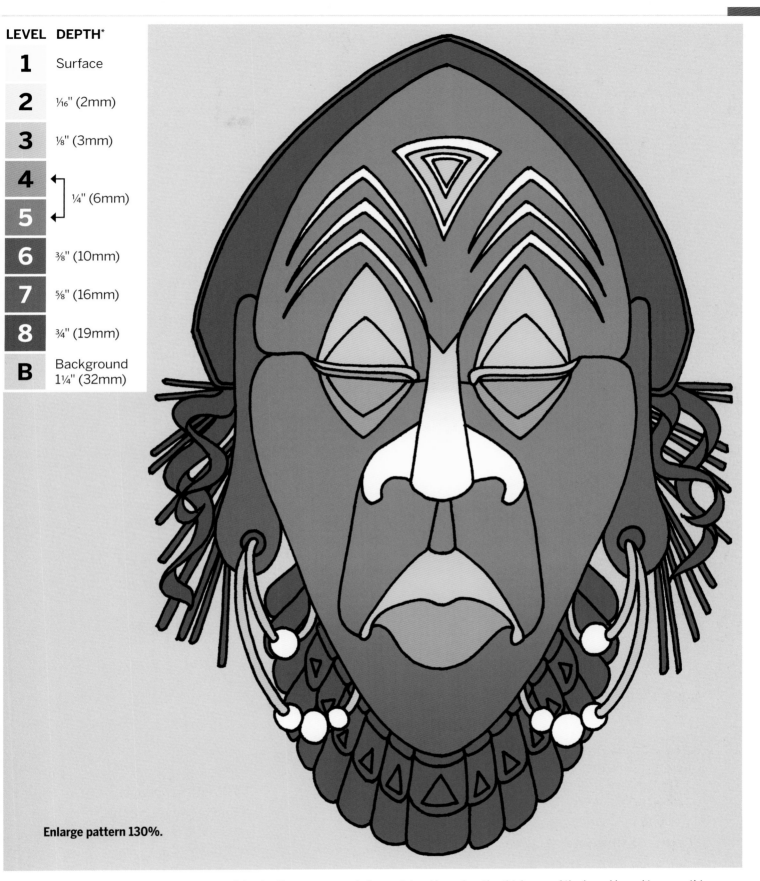

LEVEL	DEPTH*
1	Surface
2	¹⁄₁₆" (2mm)
3	⅛" (3mm)
4	¼" (6mm)
5	
6	⅜" (10mm)
7	⅝" (16mm)
8	¾" (19mm)
B	Background 1¼" (32mm)

Enlarge pattern 130%.

Note: This pattern contains rough estimates of the depth measurements for each level based on the thickness of the board I used to carve this project. Remember that relief carvings should generally be worked in the top half of your wood blank. Adjust these measurements as necessary according to the thickness of the blank you're using.

LEVEL
1
2
3
B

Note: These colored diagrams show the sub-levels of the headdress decorations and the collar. Use them for reference when carving these areas.

LEVEL

1
2
3
4
B

1 **Transfer the pattern and mark a border.** Prepare the wood blank by sanding it lightly with 220-grit sandpaper. Remove any sanding dust with a clean, dry cloth. Make a copy of the pattern, and center and tape it to the carving blank. Trace the pattern using graphite paper. To create a border, measure and mark a pencil line 2" (51mm) from the top and bottom edges of the blank. Then, measure and mark a pencil line ½" (13mm) from the bark edges. Connect these border lines at the corners, using 2"–3" (52–76mm)-diameter jar lids as a template to create curved corners.

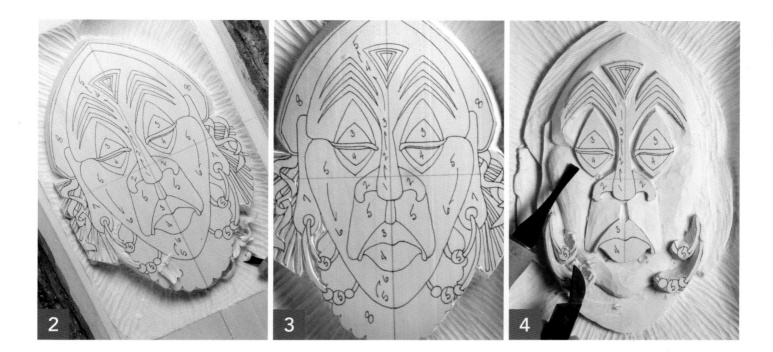

2 **Rough out the background.** Working a deep relief carving is not harder than working a standard relief carving; it simply takes longer. Create stop cuts along the outer pattern lines of the mask with a bench knife. Using a large round gouge, rough out the background. Taper the slope of the background area from the wood's original surface level at the border line to 1¼" (32mm) deep at the edge of the mask. Work this step in stages by making a stop cut and lowering the background wood to about ¼" (6mm) deep. Repeat this process until you reach your desired depth.

3 **Number the levels according to the pattern.** With a pencil, mark each level with its corresponding number on the pattern. For this pattern, eight is the lowest level, and one is the highest level. Because the blank for this carving is so thick, there is room to work one area of the pattern from one level into one or more lower levels. Note that the cheek areas of the face begin at level five near the eyes, and then drop to level six at the lower mouth corners. The highest point of the carving is the tip of the nose, at level one. The nose then drops to level three at the bridge. As you move an area or element from one level into a lower level, that level will develop the general shape of the area.

4 **Cut the elements to depth.** Make stop cuts along the pattern lines of each section of the pattern using a V-gouge or bench knife. Use a large round gouge, straight chisel, and/or bull-nose chisel to rough cut each level to its depth. At this stage, leave the facial features, facial markings, and earrings at the original level of the wood.

5 **Rough out and shape each element individually.** With deep or large carvings, work each level through each of the general carving stages separately—do the rough out work through all of the levels first, and then move on to the shaping stages. By working each stage throughout your pattern, your cutting strokes will stay more consistent.

6 **Smooth the carving and shape the earrings.** Once the rough out and general shaping stage is complete throughout the entire design, begin smoothing away the chisel and gouge ridges using a straight chisel and/or bull-nose chisel. The earring elements of the pattern were left at the original depth of the wood. Now, use your bench knife to undercut both sections of each earring. Use a large round gouge or straight chisel to remove the undercut wood. Repeat this step on both sides of the earring area to slowly work the wood out from beneath the earrings. You want to create space between the bottoms of the earrings and the wood below them. When the earrings are free-floating, cut a small strip of sandpaper to about 2" x ½" (51 x 13mm). With the grit side up, slide the sandpaper through the opening between the bottom of the earrings and the wood beneath them and smooth the bottoms of the earrings. Round over the beads on the earrings with a straight chisel.

7 **Add in the details and finish the carving.** Using a bench knife to create stop cuts and a small round chisel or tight U-gouge, define the headdress ornaments behind the ears. Use a V-gouge to make V-cuts in the decoration for the collar area. Lightly sand the carving with 220-grit sandpaper, and remove the dust with a dry, clean cloth. Apply two light coats of sanding sealer to the top carving surface of the blank, following the manufacturer's instructions. Sand after each application. Apply two light coats of polyurethane spray sealer.

PROJECT:
'No Vacancy' Birdhouse

Low Relief with Woodburning Details

Using a woodburning tool, you can add fine details to low relief carvings. Because I worked this carving on a small round-top plaque, I chose to use a woodburning tool to add in the texture and detail lines instead of a V-gouge. This kept the texture and detail lines as fine as possible.

Tools and Supplies:

- 8" x 10" x ¾" (203 x 254 x 19mm) round-top basswood plaque
- V-gouge
- Large and small round gouges
- Wide sweep round rouge
- Straight chisel
- Bull-nose chisel

- Tight U-gouge
- Bench knife or chip carving knife
- Sharpening tools and strop
- Compass
- Graphite tracing paper
- Painter's tape
- Pencil

- 220-grit sandpaper
- Variable-temperature woodburning unit
- Clean, soft cloth
- Stiff toothbrush or brass wire brush
- Thick terrycloth towel or nonslip mat

LEVEL	DEPTH
1	Surface
2	3/16" (5mm)
3	1/4" (6mm)
4	3/8" (10mm)
B	Background (3/8" (10mm))

Pattern shown at 100%.

Note: This pattern contains rough estimates of the depth measurements for each level based on the thickness of the board I used to carve this project. Remember that relief carvings should generally be worked in the top half of your wood blank. Adjust these measurements as necessary according to the thickness of the blank you're using.

Leaf patterns shown at 100%.

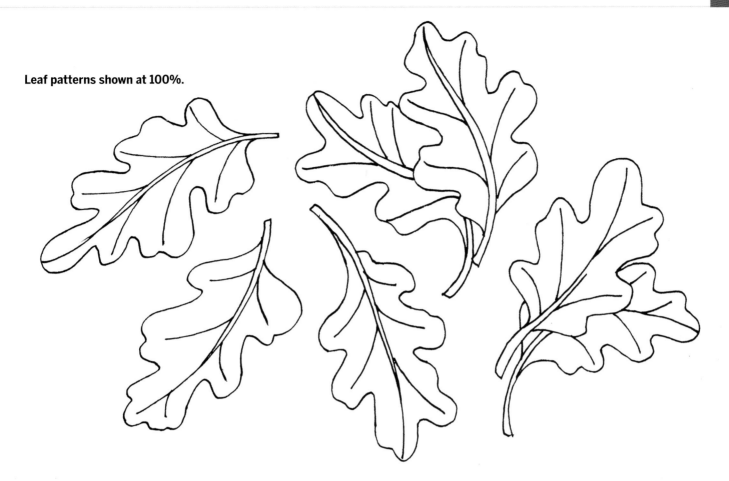

1 **Prepare the blank and transfer the pattern.**
Prepare the wood plaque by lightly sanding it with 220-grit sandpaper. Remove any dust using a soft, dry cloth. Make a copy of the pattern, and center and tape it to the board. Using graphite paper, trace the pattern.

2 **Create a border, rough out the background, and transfer the leaf patterns.** Open the legs of a compass to ½" (13mm). Place the pointed leg against the edge of the plaque with the pencil on the top of the plaque. Move the compass along the edge of the plaque to create a ½" (13mm)-wide border. Using a V-gouge and/or bench knife, create stop cuts along the outer pattern lines of the design and along the border line. With a small round gouge, rough cut the background to about ³⁄₁₆" (5mm) deep. Keep the walls of the border line as straight to the board as possible. Use your straight chisel to make the wall flat if necessary. Smooth the background area by upending your straight chisel and shaving the high ridges left by the gouge as flat as possible. Lightly sand the background using 220-grit sandpaper. Make a copy of the oak leaf pattern above. Cut the pattern into several pieces with one to two leaves on each piece. Tape the small pattern pieces to the rough cut background, arranging them around the sides of the birdhouse, and use graphite paper to trace the pattern lines.

3 **Carve the background leaves, birdhouse hole, and birdhouse front wall.** Using a V-gouge, make shallow V-cuts along the outlines of the leaves. Taper the background area into the leaves using a wide sweep round gouge or bull-nose chisel. Work the next level of the pattern—the front wall of the birdhouse—by cutting along the roof lines with a V-gouge. Taper and shape the roof area slightly with a straight chisel or bull-nose chisel. Cut the intersection between the front wall of the birdhouse and the lowest roof line with a V-gouge. Cut around the outer ring of the center hole, the bird, and the grass and perch with a V-gouge. Drop the birdhouse front wall slightly deeper than the roof area using a wide sweep round gouge or straight chisel. Drop the inside of the birdhouse hole as deeply into the wood as the background area—³⁄₁₆" (5mm) deep.

4 **Cut and shape the upper elements.** Work the upper elements, including the grass in the birdhouse hole, the perch, the sign and its string hangers, and the bird. Using a V-gouge, make stop cuts along each pattern line. Shape each element using a wide sweep gouge, straight chisel, or bull-nose chisel. The highest area is the bird's wing. Create a few undercuts in this area to add some dark shadows. Use the photo as a reference to see where undercuts have been worked under the grass, perch branches, sign, and the right side of the bird's tail. Make the undercuts with a bench knife and a straight chisel or bull-nose chisel. Lightly sand the carving using 220-grit sandpaper.

5 **Select a woodburner.** There are several varieties of woodburning units available to the woodcarver. The one shown here is an inexpensive variable-temperature unit that has interchangeable burning tips. Woodburners of this style are readily available at most craft stores.

6 **Woodburn the details.** To burn in the details for this carving, I set my woodburning unit to a medium temperature setting and used the universal tip. As you work this step, you will see that as the tool's tip burns a dark-colored line on the wood, it also burns a trough into the wood. Because of this, woodburning the detail lines gives the same V-cut effect as cutting the lines with a V-gouge, but allows for much finer lines. Your burned strokes can be varied by using the different tips that come with the unit, changing the pressure that you apply to the burn stroke, and adjusting the heat setting. Woodburning a carving not only adds extremely fine detail lines, it also burns away any loose or rough wood fibers. In this carving, the background area is very tight—too tight to create a smooth cutting stroke between the board margin area and the bird house. Woodburning tips, however, easily reach into these areas so you can add the leaf veining and background textures, and clean the edges between the two.

7 **Clean up the carving.** After the woodburning is complete, lightly sand the carving with 220-grit sandpaper to remove any remaining loose wood fibers from the work. Remove the sanding dust using a soft, dry cloth.

Painting your project

Because this carving has been woodburned, it needs to be painted to hide the unevenness of the burned lines. Begin by mixing small, equal portions of titanium white and burnt umber paint to create a medium beige color. Thin the mixture slightly with a few drops of water. Apply two even coats to the entire plaque, allowing the first coat to dry thoroughly before applying the next.

Combine small, equal portions of burnt umber paint and water. Brush one wash coat of this mixture over the entire plaque. Work this step in small areas of about 3" (76mm) square or less at a time, wiping the areas immediately with a soft, clean cloth. This gives your carving a driftwood-like, antiqued appearance. Allow this coating to dry completely (about half an hour to an hour).

On a glass tile or palette paper, mix three parts of each paint color with one part water. Apply a thin wash coat of color to each area listed below. Allow each coat to dry, and if needed, apply a second coat.

- Cadmium red medium: front roof boards, outer hole circle
- Medium verde green: top and bottom roof line, grass
- Raw sienna: bird's back, top wing area, belly at the base of the tail, acorn caps
- Titanium white: bird's belly, face cheek, sign
- Carbon black: bird's head cap, beak, top of the breast, tip of the wings, tail
- Cadmium yellow medium mixed with titanium white: sign rope
- Burnt umber: inside the birdhouse hole, acorns

To shade the background leaves, mix equal parts cadmium yellow medium and raw sienna and use this to cover the entire leaf surface. While this wash coat is still damp, add some burnt sienna, cadmium red medium, and titanium white shading.

Paint the wood of the birdhouse using the same cadmium yellow medium and raw sienna mixture you used for the leaf base. Add streaks of color with raw sienna, burnt sienna, burnt umber, and titanium white.

Add a few titanium white accents to the bird's wing feathers. Pick up a small amount of titanium white on a pencil point, and touch the point to the bird's eye to add a tiny highlight dot.

Allow the paint to dry, turn the carving to the back, and use a fine-point permanent marker to sign and date the piece. Making sure the paint is completely dry, seal the work with two light coats of polyurethane spray sealer.

Painting Supplies

- Acrylic craft paints in:
  - Burnt Umber
  - Titanium White
  - Carbon Black
  - Cadmium Red Medium
  - Raw Sienna
  - Burnt Sienna
  - Medium Verde Green
  - Cadmium Yellow Medium
- Polyurethane spray sealer
- Assorted soft-bristle paintbrushes
- Water
- Clean, soft cloth
- Glass tile, palette paper, or tinfoil
- Fine-point permanent marker

PROJECT:
Bumblebee and Sunflower

High Relief

This relief carving uses the low relief technique, with its clearly visible joint lines and rounded-over edges, for the sunflower part of the design. To make the bumblebee literally stand off the wood, so that it can fly, the bee is worked in high relief by undercutting along the wings, body, and legs.

Tools and Supplies:

- 8" x 11" x ¾" (203 x 279 x 19mm) bark-edged basswood plaque
- V-gouge
- Large and small round gouges
- Wide sweep round gouge
- Straight chisel
- Bull-nose chisel
- Tight U-gouge
- Bench knife or chip carving knife
- Variable-temperature woodburning tool
- Sharpening tools and strop
- Graphite tracing paper
- Painter's tape
- Pencil
- 220-grit sandpaper
- Soft, clean cloth
- Stiff toothbrush or brass wire brush
- Thick terrycloth towel or nonslip mat

LEVEL	DEPTH
1	Surface
2	1⁄16" (2mm)
3	1⁄8" (3mm)
4	3⁄16" (5mm)
B	Background 3⁄8" (10mm)

Note: This pattern contains rough estimates of the depth measurements for each level based on the thickness of the board I used to carve this project. Remember that relief carvings should generally be worked in the top half of your wood blank. Adjust these measurements as necessary according to the thickness of the blank you're using.

1 **Transfer the pattern, rough out the background, and carve the sunflower.** For this carving, the bee is the focal point and is the only element that is raised high above the background of the wood. The sunflower petals and center are worked as if they are part of the background area. To begin, prepare your board by lightly sanding it with 220-grit sandpaper. Remove any dust with a dry, clean cloth. Make a copy of the bee pattern, and center and tape it to the board. Using graphite paper, trace the outlines of the pattern. Rough cut the background by creating stop cuts with a V-gouge along the outer edges of the center of the sunflower and around the bee. Use a large round gouge to drop the background and the area that contains the large sunflower petals to about ⁷⁄₁₆" (11mm) deep, with the deepest point of the carving at the top edge of the sunflower's center. Retrace the sunflower petals on the board. Using a V-gouge, make stop cuts along each sunflower petal in the background area. Drop the surrounding background area that intersects with these petals another ¹⁄₁₆" (2mm). Begin rounding over the top and side of the sunflower center with a straight chisel or wide sweep gouge.

2 **Carve the sunflower's center.** To create the small center flowers, upend a large round gouge and cut a circle outline for each petal. Each small flower has five to six petals. Lower the area around the small flowers slightly using a large round gouge or straight chisel. Upend a large round gouge and use it to cut circle outlines for the centers of the small flowers. Using a small round gouge, cut a few gouge strokes in the petals to shape them and to lower the base of the petals where they connect to the flower centers. Make a copy of the pattern. Cut out the center area of the large sunflower from the pattern printout and trace the seeds onto the carving. Using your V-gouge, make V-cuts along the pattern lines for the seeds. Cut two or three small indents in the seed area to imply that several seeds have already fallen out. Using a V-gouge, make tightly packed, very shallow V-cuts in the background area of the large sunflower's center. Work from the seeds and around the small flowers to the outer edges of the large flower's center to create the lined texture.

3 **Shape the bee and flower petals.** Now, both the flower petals and the body of the bee are ready for some simple shaping. Recut V-cuts using a V-gouge along the outlines of the petals. Use a large round gouge, wide sweep gouge, or bull-nose chisel to smooth the background near the petals. With a large round gouge or straight chisel, taper each petal along the sides to tuck it under its adjacent, overhanging petal. Using a bench knife and a small round gouge or straight chisel, recut along the edges of the petals, where possible, to create undercuts. Some background space falls between the petals where they connect to the flower's center. Stop cut along these spaces using a bench knife. Lower the depth inside the spaces with a small round gouge or tight U-gouge, lowering them to the same depth as the deepest point in the background area. Recut the edges of these areas with a bench knife and small gouge to undercut each petal. Make medium-depth V-cuts in each petal with a V-gouge. Begin the general shaping of the bee's body by rounding over the three body sections of the bee with a straight chisel. Lower the inner edge of each wing so that the wing falls below the center body area.

4 **Undercut the bee's body and smooth the background and sunflower.** I decided I wanted the bee's body to be heavily undercut so that it would cast shadows onto the petals below. Work undercuts around the bee's body. Then, smooth the background area and sunflower. Using a large round gouge, wide sweep gouge, or bull-nose chisel, shave the gouge ridges left from the rough out stage to create an even background. Lightly sand the background area, including the sunflower petals, with 220-grit sandpaper.

5 Continue shaping the bee. Return to shaping the bee's body using the straight chisel and wide sweep gouge. Create a bend in the bee's legs by tapering the legs downward on either side of the center knee joint with a straight chisel, making the knee joint the high point of the leg. Undercut the large back body section and all the wing edges using a bench knife and a straight chisel or small round gouge. Round over the antenna.

6 Carve the details. Create the leg segments by upending a V-gouge to make outline cuts along the sides of the legs. Then, use a straight chisel to lower the next leg segment, working away from the knee joint. Section the body, back, and head, using a V-gouge to make V-cuts across the body to divide each section. Use the V-gouge to cut shallow, tightly packed lines, creating the fuzz of the bee's body. Use a pencil to mark the placement of the veining in the wings. Cut the veins with shallow V-cut lines. Along the outer edge of the sunflower's center, upend a V-gouge and cut small V-shaped sections from the edge. Use a bench knife or small round gouge to free the V-cut chips. With a stiff toothbrush or brass wire brush, remove any remaining loose wood fibers.

7 Woodburn the fine details. To add to the fine detailing, I chose to use my variable-temperature woodburning tool on a medium to medium/high temperature setting and with the universal tip. I used the woodburner to enhance the fine lines in the sunflower's center and in the bee's fuzz texture. Because the universal tip of the burner is V-shaped, I worked the tip in a touch-and-lift stroke around the flower's center to deepen the small V-gouge profile cuts. When you are finished woodburning the details, clean your carving well by scrubbing it with a stiff toothbrush to remove any remaining loose wood fibers.

Painting your project

To prevent the surface of the basswood from absorbing too much color, give your carving one to two light coats of polyurethane spray sealer. Allow this to dry well.

Cut several long strips of tape and place them ¼" (6m) in from the bark edges of the carving to keep this area free of paint.

Place a small amount of each color on a glass tile. Thin the paint slightly with a few drops of water. Using one to two coats of color, begin applying the color for full solid coverage, starting with the background and working toward the high areas of the carving. Apply the following colors to the following areas:

- Background sky: Mix three parts titanium white with one part ultramarine blue. Shade some areas of the sky by adding a small drop of cadmium red medium to the mix to create a soft purple-blue tone.
- Sunflower petals: Mix three parts cadmium yellow medium with one part titanium white. Shade the flower petals at the flower's center by adding a small drop of cadmium orange medium to the mix. Shade the four bottom left petals with the orange mixture. Repeat, adding a small drop of cadmium red medium to the mix.
- Bee's body and wings: Mix three parts cadmium yellow medium with one part titanium white. Highlight the fuzz of the body sections and the bottom edges of the wings with titanium white. Add carbon black to the large bottom body section, center body section, the legs, the head, and the antennae.
- Sunflower's center: Mix three parts cadmium yellow medium with one part titanium white. Shade the flower's center by adding a small drop of medium verde green to the mix and using it to paint the outer half of the flower's center. Repeat, adding another small drop of medium verde green to darken the outer quarter of the flower's center.

- Small center flowers and seeds: Shade the small flowers with a few brushstrokes of pure titanium white. Accent a few seeds in the same manner. Using the point of a pencil, pick up a small drop of the orange-red petal mixture and touch that in small dots to the inside of each small flower's center.

Remove the tape from the edges of the carving. Allow the paint to dry well (several hours or overnight). Apply two coats of polyurethane spray sealer to the entire surface of the carving. Following the manufacturer's instructions, antique the carving with a burnt umber oil stain, removing as much stain as possible with a soft dry cloth. Allow the stain to dry well—at least overnight—and then reapply one to two coats of polyurethane spray sealer.

Painting Supplies

- Acrylic craft paints in:
  - Titanium White
  - Cadmium Yellow Medium
  - Cadmium Orange Medium
  - Cadmium Red Medium
  - Ultramarine Blue
  - Medium Verde Green
  - Carbon Black
- Burnt umber oil stain
- Polyurethane spray sealer
- Painter's tape or transparent tape
- Glass tile, palette paper, or tinfoil
- Assorted soft-bristle paintbrushes
- Water
- Soft, clean cloth

Index

Note: Page numbers in *italics* indicate projects

acquisition editor **Peg Couch**   copy editor **Colleen Dorsey**   cover and page designer **Jason Deller**   editor **Katie Weeber**   indexer **Jay Kreider**
layout designer **Maura Zimmer**   project photographer **Scott Kriner**   proofreader **Lynda Jo Runkle**   senior managing editor **Paul Hambke**

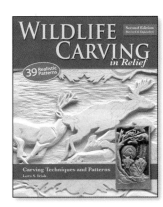
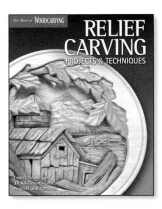
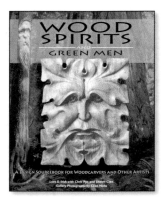
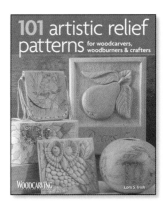